Sexualisation

Series Editor: Cara Acred

Volume 310

Independent  Publishers

First published by Independence Educational Publishers

The Studio, High Green

Great Shelford

Cambridge CB22 5EG

England

© Independence 2017

ISBN-13: 978 1 86168 760 9

Printed in Great Britain

Zenith Print Group

Contents

Introduction

Sexualisation is Volume 310 in the **ISSUES** series. The aim of the series is to offer current, diverse information about important issues in our world, from a UK perspective.

ABOUT TITLE

The sexualisation of society continues to affect people of all ages and backgrounds. This book looks at the sexualised aspects of advertising, the music industry and the fashion industry. It also considers how sexualisation is impacting our young people, asking questions such as 'When is it appropriate for girls to start wearing make-up?', 'Why are teenagers sending so many nude selfies?' and 'Are children becoming desensitised to porn?'.

OUR SOURCES

Titles in the **ISSUES** series are designed to function as educational resource books, providing a balanced overview of a specific subject.

The information in our books is comprised of facts, articles and opinions from many different sources, including:

⇨ Newspaper reports and opinion pieces

⇨ Website factsheets

⇨ Magazine and journal articles

⇨ Statistics and surveys

⇨ Government reports

⇨ Literature from special interest groups.

A NOTE ON CRITICAL EVALUATION

Because the information reprinted here is from a number of different sources, readers should bear in mind the origin of the text and whether the source is likely to have a particular bias when presenting information (or when conducting their research). It is hoped that, as you read about the many aspects of the issues explored in this book, you will critically evaluate the information presented.

It is important that you decide whether you are being presented with facts or opinions. Does the writer give a biased or unbiased report? If an opinion is being expressed, do you agree with the writer? Is there potential bias to the 'facts' or statistics behind an article?

ASSIGNMENTS

In the back of this book, you will find a selection of assignments designed to help you engage with the articles you have been reading and to explore your own opinions. Some tasks will take longer than others and there is a mixture of design, writing and research-based activities that you can complete alone or in a group.

Useful weblinks

www.bishuk.com

www.christian.org.uk

www.theconversation.com

www.develop-online.net

www.ditchthelabel.org

www.esrc.ac.uk

www.theedgesusu.co.uk

www.fullfact.org

www.theguardian.com

www.hemeltoday.co.uk

www.huffingtonpost.co.uk

www.ibtimes.co.uk

www.independent.co.uk

www.mintel.com

www.nspcc.org.uk

www.parliament.uk

researchbriefings.parliament.uk

www.somersetcoutnrygazette.co.uk

www.telegraph.co.uk

www.voice-online.co.uk

www.wired-gov.net

www.womenssupportproject.co.uk

www.yougov.co.uk

FURTHER RESEARCH

At the end of each article we have listed its source and a website that you can visit if you would like to conduct your own research. Please remember to critically evaluate any sources that you consult and consider whether the information you are viewing is accurate and unbiased.

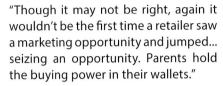

Sexualisation

What is sexualisation?

In 2007 the American Psychological Association (APA) carried out an extensive review of the impact of sexualisation on young girls. The APA's taskforce provides the following definition of sexualisation as occurring when:

⇨ a person's value comes only from his or her sexual appeal or behaviour, to the exclusion of other characteristics

⇨ a person is held to a standard that equates physical attractiveness with being sexy

⇨ a person is sexually objectified and made into a thing for others' sexual use rather than seen as a person with the capacity for independent action and decision making

⇨ sexuality is inappropriately imposed upon a person.

'Report of the APA Task Force on the Sexualisation of Girls.' American Psychological Association. Zurbriggen et al. (2007)

http://www.apa.org/pi/wpo/ sexualization.html

Why is it happening?

"We know from our research that commercial pressures towards premature sexualisation and unprincipled advertising are damaging children's well-being. The evidence shows that adults feel children are more materialistic than in past generations, while children themselves feel under pressure to keep up with the latest trends."

Penny Nicholls, director of children and young people at The Children's Society.

http://news.bbc.co.uk/1/hi uk/8619329.stm

"Though it may not be right, again it wouldn't be the first time a retailer saw a marketing opportunity and jumped... seizing an opportunity. Parents hold the buying power in their wallets."

By Lydia Dishman

http://www.bnet.com/blog/publishing-style/abercrombiespadded-bikinis-for-tweens-prove-theres-nothing-new-under-the-retail-sun/1609

How is it happening?

"How have sex, sexiness and sexualisation gained such favour in recent years as to be the measure by which women's and girls' worth is judged? While it is not a new phenomenon by any means, there is something different about the way it occurs today and how it impacts on younger and younger girls."

McLellan, 'Sexualised and Trivialized – Making Equality Impossible'. Quoted in 'Getting Real', Tankard Reist (2010)

Researchers looked at 15 websites of popular clothing stores, ranging from bargain to high-end sectors of the junior US market. Clothing was rated according to whether it had only child-like characteristics, revealed or emphasised an intimate body part, or had characteristics that were associated with sexiness.

⇨ 69% of the clothing assessed in the study had only child-like characteristics

⇨ 4% had only sexualising characteristics, while

⇨ 25% had both sexualising and child-like characteristics

⇨ 1% had neither sexualised nor child-like characteristics.

Goodin S et al. (2011). 'Putting On Sexiness: a content analysis of the presence of sexualizing characteristics

in girls' clothing.' Sex Roles; DOI:10.1007/ s11199-011-9966-8 © 2011 AFP

"Boys don't have to look hard for examples of the tough guy in popular culture – he is seen all over the television dial, in advertising, and in the books based on popular TV series. He is held up as a sort of ideal (in sharp contrast to 'wimpy' smart guy characters) and he teaches boys that success comes from being aggressive. Increasingly, the influence of this character can be seen in boys' clothing. As the examples below demonstrate, scary imagery, with its undertones of aggression, appears on clothing marketed to boys aged one and up."

http://www.achilleseffect. com/2011/01/boys-clothing-valuing- toughness-andaggression/

"Fashions like these dovetail perfectly with the messages delivered by film, television, books, and toy advertising, telling boys on the one hand that aggression and toughness are cool and, on the other, that rowdiness and bad behaviour are funny and even expected from boys."

http://www.achilleseffect. com/2011/01/boys%E2%80%99- clothing-part-2%E2%80%94the-brat/

What are the impacts?

"It is important to analyse cultural representations of gender roles, sexuality and relationships and ask what specific values are being promoted and if these are having a negative impact on child development. Key questions include the impact on children... of stereotyped images of passivity and sexual objectification... the long term impacts of early exposure to adult sexual themes and the ways in which cultural exposure impacts on parents' roles in protecting and educating children around sexuality in a developmentally appropriate way."

Newman, 'The Psychological and Developmental Impact of Sexualisation on Children'. Quoted in 'Getting Real,' Tankard Reist (2010)

"When girls are dressed to resemble adult women... adults may project adult motives as well as an adult level of responsibility and agency on girls. Images of precocious sexuality in girls may serve to normalize abusive practices such as child abuse, child prostitution, and the sexual trafficking of children... the sexualisation of girls may also contribute to a market for sex with children through the cultivation of new desires and experiences."

American Psychological Association Taskforce on the Sexualisation of Girls reported in 2007:p 35

"When we allow our young girls' childhood to be about being sexy, we take their attention away from developing their true sense of self and how they can affect the world and we put it on what others want them to be and what the world demands of them."

"It can be tempting to think that girls are taking the brunt, that boys have it easier. But in some ways the messages we are sending out to boys are just as limiting and restrictive: be macho, be strong, don't show your emotions. Hyper-sexualisation of femininity cannot exist without hypermasculinisation of males. They feed off and reinforce each other."

Dr Linda Papadopoulos, Sexualisation Review 2010

What can we do to help?

Parents/carers have an important role to play with CYP. We have to be proactive in building their resilience to these messages by talking openly and building strong, open and trusting relationships with CYP, where they know we value and support them.

Talk to your kids

Help CYP to understand that adverts and messages that link happiness and love with beauty are telling them a lie to sell products. Advertisers feed off insecurities and our need for acceptance by our peers to make us feel worse about ourselves so we will buy whatever products they tell us will make us happy and successful.

Be real

Help CYP build strengths that will allow them to achieve their goals and develop into healthy adults. Remind your children that everyone is unique and that it's unhelpful to judge people solely by their gender, clothing and appearance.

Keep telling your kids from a young age that they are loved for who they are and not how they look

Teach girls to value themselves for who they are, rather than how they look. Teach boys to value girls as friends, sisters and girlfriends, rather than as sexual objects. Encourage both genders to develop, follow interests and get involved in a sport or other activity that emphasises talents, skills and abilities over physical appearance.

Sex and relationships education

Many parents are not that comfortable talking about sex and sexuality but it's important. It should be started when they are very young. Always tell them that you are pleased they ask questions but take time to find the answers if you need to. Tell them that you think sex is OK as part of a healthy, intimate, mature relationship and that the media, peers and our culture has a big part to play in our sexual behaviours and decisions, how to make safe choices, and what makes healthy relationships.

Tune in

Minimise their exposure to commercial media and be aware of the content of all they watch, including computer games. Watch TV and movies with your children. Read their magazines. Look at their web sites. Ask questions. "Why do you think there is so much pressure on girls to look a certain way?" "What do you like most about the girls you want to spend time with?" "Do these qualities matter more than how they look?" "What do you think of the different roles that are usually given to boys and girls?" "Do you think women and men are portrayed fairly?" Really listen to what your kids tell you.

Speak up

If you don't like a TV show, CD, a music video, pair of jeans, or doll, say why. A conversation and explanation with children about the issue will be more effective than simply saying, "No, you can't buy it or watch it."

The majority of people believe that children's exposure to pornography is a significant problem and that we should do something about it. Which of the following should we do regarding sex education classes in schools? Tick all that apply.

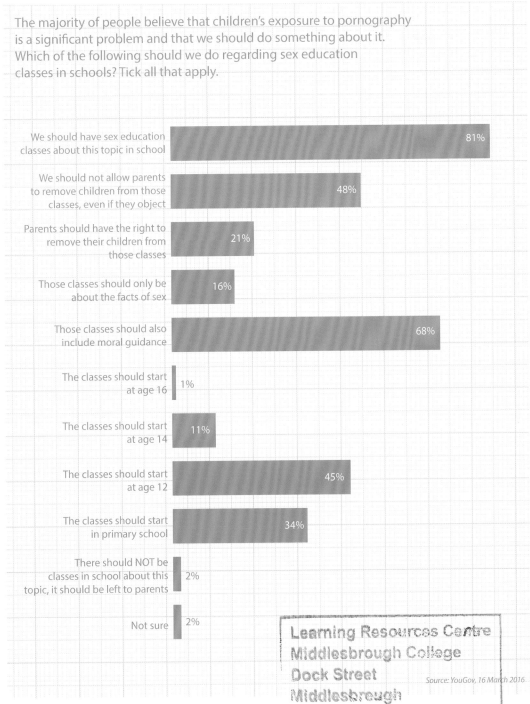

Response	%
We should have sex education classes about this topic in school	81%
We should not allow parents to remove children from those classes, even if they object	48%
Parents should have the right to remove their children from those classes	21%
Those classes should only be about the facts of sex	16%
Those classes should also include moral guidance	68%
The classes should start at age 16	1%
The classes should start at age 14	11%
The classes should start at age 12	45%
The classes should start in primary school	34%
There should NOT be classes in school about this topic, it should be left to parents	2%
Not sure	2%

Source: YouGov, 16 March 2016

image, and their son's attitudes towards women. The way men treat and talk about women in the family and women in general is a powerful model for their children. You need to consider this and how it may impact on your kids. Talk about whom you admire and hold in high regard, not just because they are rich, thin or appear as a celebrity in magazines. This helps your child understand how people demonstrate real worth in the world.

Spending power

Parents should not buy products that promote sexualisation. Think about the clothes you buy for your kids. Avoid anything that is 'mini-adult' such as skimpy underwear or bras for pre-teens.

Get involved

However, even if you make a stand against this, there could still be pester power because "everyone else has one." If we all stand up and boycott the shops that continue to sell sexualised clothing for children, things could change. You could join lobbying and influence the Government to stop the sale of such products in the UK. Support campaigns, companies and products that promote positive images of girls. Complain to manufacturers, advertisers, television and movie producers, and retail stores when products sexualise girls.

June 2015

⇨ The above information is reprinted with kind permission from Women's Support Project. Please visit www.womenssupportproject.co.uk for further information.

© Women's Support Project 2017

Try to see it their way

Remember that young people can be under a lot of pressure to conform and fit in with their peers. They can have less space to make individual choices and find alternatives. Keep in mind that clothes are an important social code for young people and their group identity. You need to work alongside them to find compromises and reassure them that looks are not everything.

Question choices

Girls who are focused on their appearance can find it difficult to concentrate on anything else. If your daughter wants to wear something you consider too sexy, ask what she likes about the outfit. Ask if there's anything she doesn't like about it. Find out why she wants to look a certain way. Rather than making judgments yourself, ask her to think about the way clothes can sexualise a person. Remember that looking different and reacting against adults may all be part of her growing up but you need to draw boundaries and talk these over with her.

Role models

Fathers are important in the development of their daughter's self-

Sexualised girls are seen as less intelligent and less worthy of help than their peers

An article from The Conversation.

THE CONVERSATION

By Elise Holland, Postdoctoral Research Fellow, University of Melbourne and Nick Haslam, Professor of Psychology, University of Melbourne.

Over the past decade, the sexualisation of children has become a fiercely debated topic around the globe, with national inquiries recently conducted in the United States, Australia and the United Kingdom.

We've also seen some spectacular retail fails. In 2006, UK chain store Tesco advertised a pole dancing kit in its toys and games section, labelled as suitable for children aged 11 years and up. In 2009, British bookstore WH Smith stocked a selection of Playboy-branded stationery products, marketed to school-age girls. And in 2011, US clothing label Abercrombie & Fitch released a range of push-up bikinis in their children's line, said to be appropriate for girls as young as eight years old. Each of these products was eventually recalled following public outrage.

This sexualisation not only impacts on how young girls see themselves, our new research shows it also affects how they are treated and viewed by adults.

Past research suggests Australian girls as young as six years old place a similar emphasis on their physical appearance as adult women. Among young girls, this self-objectification brings about a number of negative psychological outcomes, including disordered eating, anxiety, and depression.

This research reveals how many girls perceive themselves in our culture. But very little research has asked how sexualisation affects the way in which young girls are perceived by others. One recent study found that people who viewed a photo of a ten-year old girl in highly sexualised clothing (a short dress and leopard print cardigan) rated her as less intelligent and less moral than people who viewed her in less sexualised clothing.

A large body of research suggests that when adult women are depicted in sexualised clothing, they are seen as less fully human. Studies have shown that sexualised women are viewed as having lesser minds (less capacity for thoughts and intentions), and are considered less worthy of moral consideration and treatment.

In our new paper, published in the journal *Psychology of Women Quarterly*, we examined whether young girls who are presented in sexualised ways are perceived in the same, object-like manner.

In one study, we presented participants with images of women and prepubescent girls, either dressed in regular clothing or a bikini. We found that young girls were objectified – viewed as having less mental capacity and as less worthy of moral consideration – when wearing bikinis. They were objectified to a similar extent as adult women.

In our second study, we explored some potential implications of these objectifying perceptions of young girls.

Existing research suggests that objectification contributes to negative and unsympathetic responses towards adult women. One study, for instance, found that scantily clad female rape victims were seen as less deserving of moral concern relative to conservatively dressed victims, and were held to be more responsible for the rape. We wanted to gauge whether objectification had similarly damaging implications for perceptions of children.

In the study, participants viewed a photo of a girl, either wearing a black bikini or a black sundress. They were then presented with a short scenario in which she was described as being the target of bullying at school.

Once again, we found that when the young girl was depicted in a bikini, she was perceived as lacking mental capacities and as less worthy of moral treatment. Study participants blamed the bikini-clad girl more for the bullying than the sundress-wearing girl, and they were less concerned that she had been bullied.

Interestingly, participants didn't think that one girl would suffer less than the other from the bullying. They simply cared less about the welfare of the girl when she was portrayed in an objectified way.

These research findings add considerable weight to public concern over the sexualisation of children. Beyond being increasingly rampant and having destructive effects on how young girls see themselves, sexualisation negatively influences how they are perceived and treated by adults. Before girls even reach sexual maturity they are susceptible to objectifying perceptions, and the resulting view that their experiences do not matter.

With this in mind, it is important that we remain vigilant against sexualised depictions of young girls in the media, and in the marketing of age-inappropriate products. Concerns over objectification tend to focus on adult women, but children can be objectified as well, with equally troubling implications.

28 August 2015

⇨ The above information is reprinted with kind permission from *The Conversation*. Please visit www.theconversation.com for further information.

"Let children be children," says former No.10 policy chief

The failure of adults to enforce sensible boundaries online is to blame for children's warped view of sex and relationships, according to David Cameron's former policy adviser.

Steve Hilton has warned that children are being allowed to "experience the adult world too soon because we're too lazy or too weak to properly invigilate".

The result, he says, is a culture where girls think they have to look like pornography actresses and boys lose "any moral or cultural restraint to treat girls with respect or affection".

Mocking culture

Hilton wrote: "Our culture mocks the notion of childhood innocence. We don't treat children like children any more. We treat them like something they're not: adults."

And he cautioned that "premature sexualisation gives children incorrect notions of healthy sex and relationship dynamics".

Accepting that Internet-connected devices "have brought entertainment and education", he also warned that they have "erased the boundaries between the child and adult worlds".

Unhealthy sexual norms

The Prime Minister's former strategy adviser, who worked in Downing Street until 2012, said: "We need to better police the border between children and technology, because unconstrained access to the Internet prematurely exposes children to unhealthy sexual norms and disturbs normal social interactions."

> **"Our culture mocks the notion of childhood innocence. We don't treat children like children any more. We treat them like something they're not: adults"**

"Let's not blame 'kids today' for these trends," he said, adding that it was adults' fault for "failing to set up" sensible boundaries.

Hilton called for a ban on smartphones and tablets for children to "protect under-16s from unsupervised content".

"They need the freedom to play, to interact in the world, to discover themselves. They don't need the freedom to roam the internet," he concluded.

26 May 2016

⇨ The above information is reprinted with kind permission from The Christian Institute. Please visit www.christian.org.uk for further information.

My make-up battle with my little girl

By Angela Epstein

There are few things in life I can claim to have in common with Katie Price.

Well, I did once make it as a centrefold. But that was because a choir I used to sing with was featured in the middle pages of a local newspaper.

Anyway, the staples blocked out my vitals. What we do share, however, is the experience of having a young daughter who has been caught with her fingers in the cosmetic cake tin.

The difference is that while the 37-year-old model endorses her little girl's unreconstructed use of hot pink lipstick and spider leg mascara, I don't. Instead I have to battle with my 11-year-old daughter, Sophie, who feels that it's perfectly normal to dust her peachy young skin with blusher (or "blush" as she calls it) and clog her lash line with clumps of kohl.

Katie Price continues to defy critics, after being spotted leaving the New Victoria Theatre in Woking the other night with her daughter Princess Tiaamii caked in make-up Indeed she has posted a defiant video on Instagram in which her feisty youngster defends herself. ("By the way, I want to do my make-up, not my mum. I do. And anyway, it's none of your beeswax! So oosh!") Oosh, indeed.

It may well be that Price's endorsement of her daughter's painted pout is little more than an extension of the commercially lucrative narcissism on which she has built her own career. But for normal mums down here on Planet Earth, the challenge of pre-pubescent daughters wanting to wear make-up remains an enduring issue.

My own little girl deploys slightly more subtle tactics when she tries to leave the house with a dash of war paint. Sophie will wait until the very last minute before we go out (ooh, somewhere exciting like Sainsbury's or an inevitable dawdle round Claire's Accessories) before coming downstairs, running to get her coat and leaping into the car.

What she doesn't factor into her rather 007 manoeuvre is that her mother's antennae twitch at the first whiff of strawberry powder colliding with her soft, flawless face. We then go through a now well-worn ritual in which Sophie is dispatched upstairs and told to take the make-up off. Which, after robust resistance – but thankfully minus Princess's attitude – she does.

Of course you may wonder where she's getting her cosmetics from. To my knowledge there's no gumshoe pre-teen pedalling Rimmel at pocket money prices. Instead Sophie either squirrels away old bits of lipstick and eyeshadow from my own burgeoning selection. Or she collects magazine free gifts (both hers and mine).

Unlike Jordan, the price, however, is never right. Not that the model and her daughter are alone in gilding the lily. Thanks to that heinous State-side import known as the beauty pageant, legions of little girls are spray-painted like little Lolita's to prove, ironically, how pretty they are. There's no doubt little girls are growing up quicker too.

A survey last year by online retailer Escentual.com, found that more girls than ever are starting to wear make-up from the age of 11 – three years younger than it was a decade ago. The reasons are doubtless multi-factorial. To begin with, the onset of puberty in girls was 14.6 years in 1920, compared to 10.5 in 2010.

> ## "Aside from peer pressure, there's reality television and social media which drip feed images of painted perfection onto the screens of little girls already acutely aware of their appearance"

Research, including a study last year by Plymouth University, constantly flags up the link between obesity and puberty: it's thought excess weight triggers fast hormonal changes in children's bodies. Meanwhile, aside from peer pressure, there's reality television and social media which drip feed images of painted perfection onto the screens of little girls already acutely aware of their appearance.

So what's the answer? As a mother, I could arrange a make-up amnesty – with or without Sophie's compliance. Just sweep away those tacky bits of lipstick and sky blue eyeliners she secretes in her bedroom and throw them into the bin.

The irony is I have no problem with her playing with make-up. For little girls, it's a rite of passage. I did it myself (although in a limited way, since my late mum's cosmetic collection extended little beyond a coral lipstick and some creamy 'rouge').

But allowing her to leave the house wearing make-up at this tender age would both ritualise and normalise it. And I'm simply not prepared to do that.

I can already see my little girl growing up in so many ways – and I want to encourage her imagination and independence. We just don't need a slick of lipstick to sign off her childhood just yet.

Of course Queen Katie and her princess may disagree. But then it's none of their beeswax. Pity this mother/daughter combo makes it ours.

16 December 2015

⇨ The above information is reprinted with kind permission from *The Telegraph*. Please visit www.telegraph.co.uk for further information.

Children at risk of becoming 'desensitised' to online porn

Some young people want to copy what they see in online porn – but they also said it doesn't teach consent.

Our survey of more than 1,000 children aged 11–16 found that at least half had been exposed to online porn. Almost all (94%) of this group have seen it by age 14. We joined forces with the Children's Commissioner for England to commission research by Middlesex University into the impact of online porn on young people, in the largest study of its kind.

Boys in particular wanted to copy some of the behaviour they had seen watching online porn. More than a third (39%) of 13- to 14-year-olds who responded to this question – and a fifth of 11- to 12-year-olds (21%) – wanted to do this. This was despite more than three quarters of respondents agreeing that pornography did not help them understand consent.

The survey revealed that young people are as likely to see online porn accidentally as they are to actively search for it, with a quarter having received online links. The first exposure to porn was at home for almost two-thirds of children.

Just over half of boys (53%) believed that the pornography they had seen was realistic compared to 39% of girls. A number of girls said they were worried about how porn would make boys see girls and the possible impact on attitudes to sex and relationships.

"It can make a boy not look for love, just look for sex and it can pressure us girls to act and look and behave in a certain way before we might be ready for it"

13-year-old girl

Children also described how their feelings towards porn change over time. 27% of the young people surveyed reported feeling "shocked"

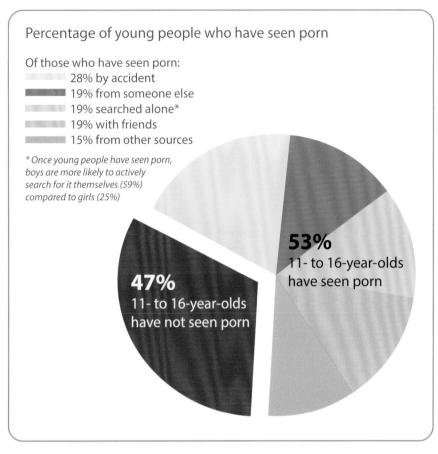

Percentage of young people who have seen porn

Of those who have seen porn:
- 28% by accident
- 19% from someone else
- 19% searched alone*
- 19% with friends
- 15% from other sources

* Once young people have seen porn, boys are more likely to actively search for it themselves (59%) compared to girls (25%)

47% 11- to 16-year-olds have not seen porn

53% 11- to 16-year-olds have seen porn

the first time they viewed it. But follow-up work revealed that just 8% remained shocked after the first time they watched it.

As viewing porn becomes more widespread among young people, many of the children surveyed recognised that it could create a poor understanding of sex and relationships.

"A few of my friends have used it for guidance about sex and are getting the wrong image of relationships"

13-year-old girl

Many of the 11- to 16-year-olds who took part in the research stated that lessons in school which explored issues surrounding online pornography can help them have a better understanding of the importance of respectful relationships. However, they often said the sex and relationships education they received didn't cover this effectively.

"We need to ensure sex is placed in the context of loving, respectful relationships based on mutual consent. Age-appropriate sex and relationship education in schools, dealing with issues such as online pornography and children sending indecent images, is crucial."

Peter Wanless/NSPCC CEO

19 June 2016

⇨ The above information is reprinted with kind permission from the NSPCC. Please visit www.nspcc.org.uk for further information.

© NSPCC 2017

An educational guide to porn

Written by Justin Hancock

Porn does teach some stuff about sex: some of this is not bad, some of it is really terrible.

I don't think people go to porn to learn about how to have sex – just like they wouldn't learn how to drive by playing GTA. But the problem is that many of us have had pretty bad sex and relationships education so there's a gap between fantasy and reality. Also many young people haven't had sex so they don't have much real-life experience to compare it to.

So this is why I've got so many posts about porn. These are the basics. Hopefully you'll learn something, or at least LOL at the funny pictures.

They are acting

Even though they are actually having sex in porn scenes, they are acting. It's kind of like wrestling on the telly, it's all made up even though it's real. They are usually acting to make it look better than it actually feels. It's edited together to look more fun and generally more epic.

Also there is a lot more moaning and groaning in porn than in real life – again like wrestling. Some of the noises and screaming might sound like it's hurting but it's actually just overacting.

Porn norms

Some things are so common in porn that you might think it's 'normal' and that's what everyone does in real life. Remember that if you have sex it's better to think more about what you actually want, rather than having sex that you think you should have. This means that sex is consensual but also more enjoyable.

It's mostly for men

In a lot of porn the actors look at the camera rather than each other. As most porn is made for straight men the woman looks into the camera so he can imagine he's having sex with her. In porn made for women they usually don't look at the camera, studies suggest that women watching find this a lot hotter.

Even in amateur porn (where it's real couples having sex with each other and filming it), it's usually the guy holding or directing the camera. However there is porn out there which is not just aimed at men. Some porn is made by women for women but there's also a lot of porn for a diverse range of genders and sexualities.

Women in porn

Some porn can be quite negative about women. Some people think that porn shows women as passive sex objects who have no power, with no brains and who's only purpose is to have sex to please men.

Some of the story lines of porn can be negative about women, for example where women are 'tricked' into having sex. In reality these women are porn performers who are paid, but the story can be negative and unpleasant.

Also the language of porn can be negative about women and usually describes acts which are done to women rather than with them.

Porn talk

Porn is really good at showing lots of people having what looks like very pleasurable sex. However, it's really bad at teaching how to actually have really pleasurable sex. In order to have really great sex the most important thing is to work out what it is you want (and don't want) and to try and find a way to communicate this to someone else.

The only talking that happens in porn is in the script, people calling each other names and people telling each other that they are enjoying it. So it's like "you like that don't you?" rather than "does this feel good?" or "oh wow that feels good".

In porn all the communication happens off camera and so the sex they have looks really easy. All kinds of sex needs trust, patience and communication to be enjoyable.

They probably don't look like you

There are a diverse range of bodies in porn. Older, bigger, hairy, there are trans* performers, gender queer folk – although there aren't many performers with physical disabilities. However, many performers look similar – particularly those that are in the main studios.

Comparing ourselves to other people is often not a great idea but it's good to bear in mind that porn stars are meant to look like this. They are meant to:

⇨ have little or no body hair

⇨ trim or wax their pubes

⇨ have bigger than average penises

⇨ have big boobs or slim tummies (or both)

⇨ wear make up

⇨ be able to get aroused and ejaculate.

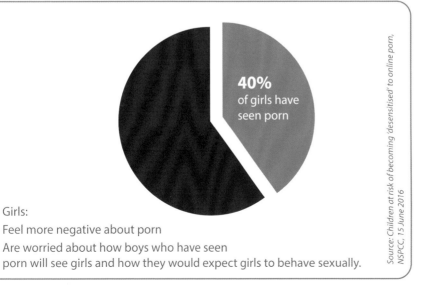

40% of girls have seen porn

Girls:
Feel more negative about porn
Are worried about how boys who have seen porn will see girls and how they would expect girls to behave sexually.

Source: Children at risk of becoming 'desensitised' to online porn, NSPCC, 15 June 2016

Condoms are rare and magical

Condoms are not often used in porn. However, most gay porn features condoms and porn studios in California (that's most of them) are now required to use them. Remember, porn actors have very regular check-ups for HIV and other STIs (usually once a month, sometimes less). They are very aware of the risks they take and some studios insist on using condoms and getting check-ups.

Porn careers

Pizza delivery guys really don't get to have sex when they are delivering pizza. Same with gardeners, milk delivery people, pool cleaners, cable installers, plumbers, secretaries, lecturers, IT people and window cleaners. I haven't read any research into which jobs are the most likely to result in having sex during the work day – but I think this is more to do with fantasy than real life. #justsayin

Porno chic

Women don't always dress up to have sex. They also don't always wear make-up or comb their hair. Many people (not just women) like to get dressed up, to look and smell nice before they have sex – but not all the time. There's a difference between looking sexy and actually feeling it. Sometimes they are the same, but often they're not. So if someone is dressed in a sexy way it doesn't mean they want to have sex.

You might not like it

If you pay any attention to the news you would think that all young people are into porn. It's just not true. Many many people of all ages are not really interested in sex and there are loads and loads of people who love having sex but hate porn.

Even people that like porn don't like everything they see. That's cool. There is a huge amount of different kinds of sex on show in porn for different people with different tastes. What's hot for one person might not be for another.

Porn mass debate

Many people think that porn is harmful. Some former porn stars have left the industry and campaign against it saying that it exploits women and hurts people watching it.

But many people think that porn is good. Women get paid more than men. Porn can show men and women positively too and can help people to explore their sexuality.

A lot of people think that there is good porn or bad porn. Or ethical and unethical use of porn.

What do you think?

1 April 2015

⇨ The above information is reprinted with kind permission from Justin Hancock of BISH. Please visit www.bishuk.com for further information.

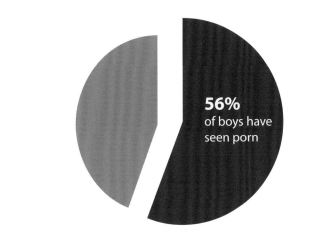

56%
of boys have seen porn

Boys:
Feel more positive about online porn
Are less likely to see online porn as exploitative, degrading or humiliating.

Source: Children at risk of becoming 'desensitised' to online porn, NSPCC, 15 June 2016

Why are young people sharing nude selfies?

Many young people are aware of the risks of sending naked selfies, but often choose to do so anyway because they see it as a fun and normal part of relationships, a study to be highlighted at the ESRC Festival of Social Science has shown.

The report found that children, some as young as 12, are sharing these photos – and for many of the study group, consisting of people who had shared naked photos under the age of 18, it was a natural way of exploring their sexuality and something they did with a trusted partner. Some, however, were coerced and threatened, often by strangers they had met online.

The research findings of *Self-Produced Images - Risk Taking Online (SPIRTO)* demonstrate the difficulties police, parents and schools face in distinguishing between normal, healthy behaviour and illegal abuse. Led by Dr Ethel Quayle at the University of Edinburgh, key findings of *SPIRTO*, which was funded by the European Union's Safer Internet Programme, included:

⇨ 73 per cent sent images because they were asked to, either by their partner or someone unknown to them. Even amongst consensual relationships, there was a level of pressure felt to please that person and to feel that they 'fitted in'. Some were asked to send photos as proof of loving their partner, and they found it hard to say no.

⇨ 59 per cent of the teens said they sent the photos because it was fun, exciting and a good way of flirting and meeting people.

⇨ 59 per cent were asked to send photos by a romantic partner – many saw it as a natural part of a relationship, which was expected of them from within their peer group.

⇨ 47 per cent said that they sent nude pictures as a way of getting attention and compliments about their looks. Girls in particular said it helped build their self-confidence.

⇨ For a minority, the need for self-affirmation had spiralled out of their control. Eight per cent described having an intense need to send images, and this was starting to affect their school work or social situation with friends.

⇨ Sending nude images did not necessarily mean the young person had started to have sex, but the images formed part of their adolescent development and allowed them to explore their sexuality.

⇨ 12 per cent described being explicitly coerced into sending nude images. Often the perpetrator threatened to share images that had already been sent with the victim's family.

Rather than making a rash decision, most of the participants carefully considered whether or not to send a naked photo of themselves. Most were aware of the risks, and often took steps to mitigate them, such as not including their face in the photo, or any clear identifying marks such as tattoos. Many kept compromising photos of the other person as a sort of mutually assured destruction.

In the majority of cases, naked selfies were not shared beyond the intended recipient.

However, 16 per cent of the young people reported that their parents and the school had found out that they sent photos, usually because the images had been found on a mobile phone. Often this had led to the youngster receiving an intervention from the police, school staff and their

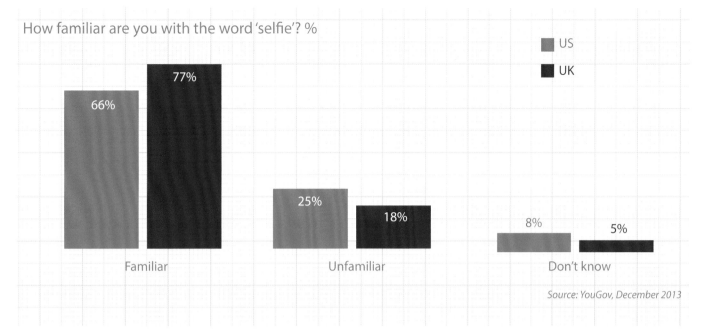

How familiar are you with the word 'selfie'? %

- US
- UK

	Familiar	Unfamiliar	Don't know
US	66%	25%	8%
UK	77%	18%	5%

Source: YouGov, December 2013

parents, which had caused intense shame and embarrassment.

22 per cent also said their selfies were shown to their peers – in several instances this led to harassment, threats or bullying and the police getting involved.

"The experiences of the young people varied from coercive online grooming where children were pressured to produce images by use of aggressive threats, to the other end of the spectrum where the images were produced in a romantic and caring relationship," says Dr Ethel Quayle. "In between we saw different levels of what might be thought of as coercion, where children felt an expectation that sending selfies is what people are doing, and if you didn't do it there was something wrong with you."

The consequences of sending the images were not always absolutely catastrophic, but they were for some people.

The problem is how do we differentiate between sexting, which we may not like or approve of but is taking place in the context of a consensual romantic relationship, from something which we really need to take seriously?

Currently there aren't any guidelines to help police and social workers deal with cases where naked selfies taken by children have been shared without their permission. Police in the UK have to investigate if there is a suggestion another person may be involved, and it is enormously resource demanding for the police.

Dr Quayle is now working with Dr Laura Cariola, a clinical psychologist at the University of Edinburgh, in a new ESRC-funded study which puts the concerns of children at the heart of policy recommendations. The young people are being asked how police, social workers, teachers and parents can help them when things go wrong – when a naked selfie is shared amongst the whole school or ends up on the Internet. The preliminary results show that simply being listened to and not judged are the most important things a parent can do to help.

"Maybe we have to accept that where it is not abused by others, the creation of images within a romantic and sexual relationship is part and parcel of growing up for some young people," says Dr Quayle. "For some groups, such as lesbian, gay and bisexual young people, it may be that this is their only route into exploring their sexuality and first relationships."

However, we need to make sure that appropriate support structures are in place for when things may go wrong.

2 November 2016

⇨ The above information is reprinted with kind permission from the Economic and Social Research Council. Please visit www.wired-gov.net for further information.

Why we must discuss sex, rape and porn in the classroom

THE CONVERSATION

An article from The Conversation.

By Heather Brunskell-Evans, Research Associate, University of Leicester

The results of a recent NSPCC Childline survey revealed the extent to which children were exposed, addicted and even making and using pornographic imagery and videos, showed how for many children and young teenagers porn is a part of everyday life. The findings may be shocking but the new social realities of the Internet and social media, and an increasingly sexualised offline and online environment, mean we must find new ways of tackling how we deal with and talk about sex.

One way to help children better understand sex and sexuality is through good sex education – but while impassioned debate continues over whether sex and relationships education (SRE) should become mandatory in schools, there is an argument for going further: for discussing porn and other issues such as rape in schools.

SRE has been proposed as just one part of the Personal and Social Health Education curriculum in schools, which aims to "cover all of the skills and knowledge young people need to manage their lives, stay safe, make the right decisions, and thrive as individuals in modern society". However, PSHE itself is currently voluntary. PSHE should be mandatory, and sexual images, sexual consent, rape myths and issues surrounding pornography should be taught in secondary schools as part of this curriculum.

Loss of innocence and state control

In an article in the *Sunday Times*, education secretary Nicky Morgan flagged up PSHE as one aspect of the struggle for gender justice and equality. Part of this was teaching girls about "what a healthy relationship looks like and how to say 'no'". But despite endorsing it for all schools, she held back from talking about SRE and instead referred to resources from "expert organisations" that were "inappropriate, explicit, or clearly at odds with fundamental British values." Instead they were working with the PSHE to develop a list of materials that would "give teachers more confidence".

But confidence of teachers is not the point here – nor avoiding issues that are clearly affecting children. Technology safety filters are clearly not effective in preventing the ubiquity of children's access to pornography. And the case can be made that if SRE is a good idea, then why is it so difficult to introduce?

Shying away from a "moral minefield"

In a recent edition of the BBC's *Moral Maze*, SRE was framed as a moral, ethical and emotional "minefield". Critics discussing the controversies broadly fell into two opposing camps. The usual case was made for the preservation of childhood innocence – that children should be spared the details of adult sexuality for as long as possible. Teaching about pornography could legitimate it and, as such, SRE would contribute to the very problem of over-sexualisation which it was partly designed to address. Another case was made that sex education was itself to blame. Young women are now more sexually confident than ever, and when they are scared of sex they don't get this fear from porn but from PSHE lessons.

The PSHE Association's report was criticised as overly concerned with women and violence and hypocritical: the definition of consent was overblown; it over-complicated human relationships; and its recommendations were

intrusive, prescriptive and conformist. If made mandatory, SRE is in danger of mobilising a state sanctioned view of what a "healthy" relationship is and is essentially an exercise in social control.

Both of these criticisms framed pornography and the industry that produced it as unstoppable facts of life, yet the misogynistic and gendered power aspects of consent, rape and pornography were left unaddressed.

Pornography in the classroom

Christian Graugaard, a Danish sexologist, has argued that pornography should be shown to 15- and 16-year-old students under controlled conditions in the classroom (since 1970, sex education has been mandatory in Denmark and pornography is part of the curriculum in some Danish schools).

He insisted that if we don't invite young people into a critical discussion about the misogynistic aspects of pornography we left them no yardsticks to make sense of sex other than those provided by the industry. Showing pornography was a sensible way of teaching teenagers that pornography is nothing like real sex. As porn is so available to teenagers, what Graugaard wanted was to make sure they "possess the necessary skills to view porn constructively" and "become conscientious and critical consumers". For Graugaard:

"Porn can even be feminist and in some cases it can be part of a democratisation of sex and [it can] promote diversity. But it can also be excluding – of body types, gender and sexuality. We want our kids to have exciting and gratifying sex lives, so an open-minded, constructive dialogue is the best way to make sure that they are able to make meaningful decisions for themselves."

The ensuing debate took the predictable dichotomous format: teaching children about pornography will destroy children's innocence, they're media savvy, and to suggest they are adversely affected by pornography is to inflate adult anxiety into a moral panic.

SRE is in part the struggle for gender justice and equality. Graugaard's proposal that showing pornography to 15- to 16-year-olds provides a forum in which this misogynistic and largely narrow medium can be visually demonstrated and critically discussed by teenagers. However, Graugaard's good porn/bad porn distinction implies that pornography is a diverse genre, yet the majority of mainstream pornography is similar and hard-core in its narrative in eroticising the dehumanisation and degradation of women.

It's our bad habit too

It's not teenage sex that should

challenge us morally; teenagers have powerful, erotic feelings which will find expression. I take the late-20th century societal worry over teenagers' smoking as something of an analogous example. It was not only hypocritical but ineffectual to tell teenagers that smoking was bad for their health. Smoking remained a rite of passage to adulthood so long as adults preserved it for their pleasure alone.

In the furore of whether we should or should not bring consent, rape and pornography into the classroom, we should perhaps dare to shine a lens on ourselves. If pornography is legitimated as a grown-up pleasure, and not seen as a problem in terms of men's (and some women's) apparent appetite for the sexual dehumanisation of women, young people will bear the burden of our legacy.

7 April 2015

⇨ The above information is reprinted with kind permission from *The Conversation*. Please visit www.theconversation.com for further information.

School dress codes reinforce the message that women's bodies are dangerous

There are far more rules about girls' clothing than boys'. When teenagers are denied classroom time it privileges their sexualisation over their right to learn.

By Laura Bates

As pupils go back to school this month, one institution has hit the headlines for sending up to 150 girls home for wearing skirts that were deemed "too short". Pupils at Tring School in Hertfordshire were either placed in seclusion or had to be picked up by their parents, reported ITV news.

A statement from Tring School's headteacher, Sue Collings, said: "We believe that students looking smart and professional is an important element of being a successful school. We also believe that, if students are consistently dressed in the correct uniform, it enables us to focus on teaching and learning. As such, we have a school uniform policy that has been in place for some time that is adhered to by the large majority of the students. The most contentious issue, though, is the style and length of the skirt worn by the girls." It also stressed that parents and pupils had been warned in advance that uniform regulations would be tightened after a decision by school leadership in the summer.

But parents commenting below the statement on the school's Facebook page expressed frustration at their struggle to find skirts that would fit their daughters' waists while fulfilling the length requirement; some said their daughters' heights or body shapes simply made the skirt sit higher. One parent commented: "My daughter wore 'regular', not skinny, trousers from a school uniform shop, they had no external pockets as per guidance and [she] was told they showed every bone in her body and was put in internal for four lessons today." On another post a parent said her daughter had been forced to wear a skirt several sizes too big safety-pinned round her waist in order to obey the length requirement.

Tring wasn't the only school to take such measures – other reports have described children being sent home from various schools in the past week for wearing the wrong footwear, or even the wrong kind of socks. But while boys have been punished for some dress code violations too, it is clear that the majority of cases involve girls' appearance being policed.

A number of pupils at South Shields Community College were made to change because their trousers were deemed "too tight". And these cases follow hot on the heels of two schools that have banned female pupils from wearing skirts altogether. In May, Bridlington School in East Yorkshire, reportedly banned skirts after a male staff member was made to feel "uncomfortable" when implementing rules over their length. And in July it was reported that Trentham High School in Stoke-on-Trent was banning skirts, with the head teacher saying: "It's not pleasant for male members of staff and students either, the girls have to walk up stairs and sit down and it's a complete distraction." This week the same school is reported to have sent home ten girls whose trousers were deemed too tight because they would prove a "distraction" to male teachers.

The media images of the Tring schoolgirls in their "inappropriate" skirts, worn over thick black tights, powerfully remind me of another recent case, in which a US teenager was sent home from school for wearing an outfit that revealed her collarbones. What is so shocking, or offensive, about the bottom inch of a teenage girl's thigh, or the bones below her neck?

In fact, that case was just the latest in a recent string of high-profile dress code battles in the US and Canada, where students have been protesting for some time about dress codes that unfairly target girls, using the hashtag #IAmMoreThanADistraction and turning up at school with placards asking: "Are my pants lowering your test scores?"

While the principle of asking students to attend school smartly dressed sounds reasonable, the problem comes when wider sexist attitudes towards women and their bodies are projected on to young women by schools in their attempt to define what constitutes smartness. It's no coincidence that many school dress codes contain far more rules

What did you learn in school today?

That the length of a skirt is more important than education!

pertaining to girls' clothing than to boys', as we live in a world where women's bodies are policed and fought over to a far greater extent than men's. When girls are denied time in the classroom because their knees, shoulders or upper arms are considered inappropriate and in need of covering up, it privileges the societal sexualisation of their adolescent bodies over their own right to learn. We don't have the same qualms about seeing those parts of their male peers' anatomy.

All this is before we can even begin to explore the potentially negative impact of draconian dress codes on trans or non-gender-conforming pupils, many of whom have reported being blocked from their school yearbooks because of clothing choices.

Another common refrain is that it is important to prepare pupils for the "world of work" – this was the explanation given by the headmaster of Ryde Academy on the Isle of Wight last year when more than 250 girls were taken out of lessons because their skirts were too short. But if schools pull girls out of lessons and publicly shame them for exposing too much of their bodies, they are only preparing them for a sexist and unfair working world in which women are constantly judged and berated on their appearance. Men, by comparison, get a free pass. Look at the endless articles about whether women "should" or "shouldn't" wear make-up to be taken seriously at work, or cringe-worthy instructions from firms on how female staff should dress.

Wouldn't it be refreshing to see a school taking a stand against the idea that girls' bodies are irresistibly dangerous and sexualised, instead of reinforcing it?

10 September 2015

⇨ The above information is reprinted with kind permission from *The Guardian*. Please visit www.theguardian.com for further information.

Sexualised behaviour in very young children increasing, say teachers

Sex and relationship education currently inadequate in context of sexual material freely available online, which may be leading to rise in sexual assaults.

By Karen McVeigh and Sarah Marsh

There is a "slow creep" of sexualised language and behaviour among children as young as five in the classroom, teachers have told *The Guardian*.

Primary and secondary school teachers described the level of sex and relationship education (SRE) available to children as inadequate in response to a call out via *The Guardian*'s online Teachers Network.

Their evidence, although anecdotal, gives a troubling glimpse into classrooms where teachers are trying but failing to tackle sexual bullying, harassment and other sexual violence experienced by pupils.

One primary school teacher, based in Merseyside, reported a series of disturbing incidents in the classroom, including pupils as young as ten being sent explicit photos via social media and a sexual assault between two seven-year-old boys. A secondary school supply teacher, who has worked in London and Humberside, reported "several sexual assaults and a possible rape" over seven years of teaching.

Dozens of teachers contacted *The Guardian* in response to a call out about sexual violence in schools, shortly before the publication of the Commons select committee inquiry into the issue on Tuesday. The inquiry, begun after a study revealed that many incidents went unreported and others were "brushed off" by teachers, is expected to raise the issue of mandatory SRE, which, although widely supported, was rejected by the Government last year.

The teachers who spoke to *The Guardian* echoed concerns raised by witnesses to the inquiry, who called for children as young as four to be taught about sexism and harassment in order to tackle a "ticking timebomb" of sexual bullying at school. All said they would like to see compulsory SRE, as well as specific guidance on how to prevent sexual bullying and violence.

One primary school teacher with 20 years' experience, who works in Merseyside, said she believed unrestricted access to the Internet was partly responsible for the sexualisation of children.

Speaking on the condition of anonymity, in order to protect the children involved, she said: "As a primary teacher, I have been appalled by the rise in sexual language and behaviour in children as young as five. Unfiltered access to the Internet and age-inappropriate computer games is exposing more and more young children to things they are not able to cope with or understand. Many parents haven't got a clue what is happening."

The teacher, who works in an area with high levels of deprivation but has seen problems in schools in better off areas, said: "In the 60s and 70s, the TV was the babysitter in the corner but now it's the Internet and the Internet is a dangerous place. Children as young as five are being left on their own with access to the Internet. They seeing things they should not be exposed to and it's not being balanced by parents telling them how to keep safe."

She has noticed a "slow creep" of inappropriately sexual language and behaviour, to the point where it has become "almost commonplace" she said.

"We've had children as young as ten getting on to social media forums, where they can have conversations and then have been sent explicit photographs. We've had a sexual assault that involved two seven-year-old boys. One of them said he was copying something on TV. I've heard male children say 'let me touch your boobies' and you can see the horrified faces on some of the other children. There is a lot of use of the word 'gay' as a term of abuse."

Age-appropriate SRE was vital, she said, and should start in primary school. "You can't put the genie back in the bottle but children need to be taught about what is and isn't OK."

Teachers said the pressure on them to deliver academic results meant that teaching social skills such as respect and healthy relationships took a back seat, with disturbing results in some schools.

One secondary school supply teacher, who has worked in Humberside and London, said: "During my seven years of teaching, there have been a number of serious sexual assaults, including a possible rape. As a matter of course, this information is not openly shared among staff and, therefore, possibly allowed to continue unchecked."

He expressed concern over the fall-out after a 14-year-old girl, who broke down in his class, alleged that she had been raped by a fellow classmate. On another occasion, a female pupil accused two boys of forcing her to perform a sex act in a science cupboard in an incident that the supply teacher said was as treated as "teenage high jinks". Neither incident appeared to be treated appropriately, he said.

"I found it preposterous that the girl who had made the accusation of rape had to leave the class. She ended up leaving the school to go to another school. It blew my mind. There should be policies in place to deal with sexual assault in order for the schools to properly deal with it."

According to a BBC investigation last September, based on freedom of information requests to police, 5,500 sexual offences were recorded in UK schools over a three-year period, including rapes. A 2014 survey by Girlguiding UK found that 59% of young women aged 13–21 had faced some form of sexual harassment at school or college in the past year.

A deputy head of a secondary school in Manchester told *The Guardian* that children needed extra guidance because of the rise in social media and the availability of online pornography.

The deputy head said: "We are living in a different world. In a school, its bell to bell, the day is gone in the blink of an eye. We know it's important but you do need support to get it right. The whole basis of gender respect and healthy relationships should be on the curriculum. Our PSHE has been taken off the timetable in terms of having a regular weekly or two-weekly slot. It's now down to six days a year. That's not enough. If children were graded in how healthy and respectful their relationships [were], as well as maths and English, there would be time on the timetable for it."

The National Police Chiefs Council, in its evidence to the commons inquiry, highlighted the availability of online pornography and the absence of sex and relationship education in schools as driving factors in altering the behaviour of young people.

One secondary head of PSHE, based in Lincolnshire, told *The Guardian* that 95% of a class of Year 7 boys told her they had accessed pornography online.

Another teacher, who works in a state-funded secondary school for vulnerable children who have been excluded from mainstream school, described her job as a "tug of war". She said that for excluded or otherwise vulnerable children SRE should be on a par with maths and English. "Our children are classified as a vulnerable because they have been in gangs or because of their family or behavioural issues. There is a lot of violence in their lives. We try to teach respect and feminism but it's hard because we only have one lesson a week. We need an extra lesson every week, at least.

"In a school like ours, it's a tug of war between getting exam results and getting them into college, and teaching them life skills about how to engage in healthy relationships. It is sad because they are the ones [who] need it most."

Additional reporting by Marianna Spring.

12 September 2016

⇨ The above information is reprinted with kind permission from *The Guardian*. Please visit www.theguardian.com for further information.

"Widespread" sexual harassment and violence in schools must be tackled

Report by the Women and Equalities Committee exposes the shocking scale of sexual harassment and sexual violence that is not being tackled effectively in English schools.

The scale of sexual harassment

The report outlines evidence that:

⇨ almost a third (29%) of 16- to 18-year-old girls say they have experienced unwanted sexual touching at school

⇨ nearly three-quarters (71%) of all 16- to 18-year-old boys and girls say they hear terms such as "slut" or "slag" used towards girls at schools on a regular basis

⇨ 59% of girls and young women aged 13–21 said in 2014 that they had faced some form of sexual harassment at school or college in the past year.

Everyday Sexism Project

Young people told the Committee that sexual harassment has become a normal part of school life with "calling women bitches and stuff like that… a common thing that you see in school, on a daily basis really". This view was supported by evidence from Laura Bates of the Everyday Sexism Project who described sexual harassment and sexual violence in schools as "a widespread, regular and common problem [and] something that the majority of girls are experiencing".

The report finds an alarming inconsistency in how schools deal with sexual harassment and violence, which is mostly targeted at girls, a disregard for existing national and international equality obligations, and a lack of guidance and support for teachers.

MPs heard evidence that many schools are under-reporting incidents and often failing to take them seriously. The Committee was told by young people that their reports would be "forgotten about really easily and no action will be taken about what happened". Academics and specialists working in schools warned that sexual harassment and sexual violence was too often accepted as the norm by both staff and students.

Despite calls from parents, teachers and young people for action to address sexual harassment and sexual violence in schools, the Committee found that neither OFSTED nor the Department for Education has a coherent plan to tackle this issue and to monitor the scale of the problem.

Chair's comments

Maria Miller MP said:

"Our inquiry has revealed a concerning picture. We have heard girls talk about sexual bullying and abuse as an expected part of their everyday life; with teachers accepting sexual harassment as 'just banter'; and parents struggling to know how they can best support their children.

"It is difficult to explain why any school would allow girls to be subjected to sexual harassment and violent behaviour that has been outlawed in the adult workplace. The evidence shows it is undermining the confidence of young women. Failing to reinforce what is acceptable behaviour could well be fuelling the 'Lad Culture' that the Government has already identified as a problem in colleges and universities.

"Despite this, the Department for Education and Ofsted have no coherent plan to ensure schools tackle the causes and consequences of sexual harassment and sexual violence. There are some examples of excellent work being done by schools and third sector organisations to prevent sexual harassment and sexual violence. But too many schools are failing to recognise this as a problem and therefore failing to act.

Sexual harassment in the workplace

The 2016 *Still just a bit of banter?* report by TUC found that:

- More than half (fifty two per cent) of all women polled have experienced some form of sexual harassment.

- Thirty-five per cent of women have heard comments of a sexual nature being made about other women in the workplace.

- Thirty-two per cent of women have been subject to unwelcome jokes of a sexual nature.

- Twenty-eight per cent of women have been subject to comments of a sexual nature about their body or clothes.

- Nearly one quarter of women have experienced unwanted touching (such as a hand on the knee or lower back).

- One fifth of women have experienced unwanted sexual advances.

- More than one in ten women reported experiencing unwanted sexual touching or attempts to kiss them.

- In the vast majority of cases, the perpetrator was a male colleague, with nearly one in five reporting that their direct manager or someone else with direct authority over them was the perpetrator.

- Four out of five women did not report the sexual harassment to their employer.

"The Government must take a lead and make it clear that sexual harassment in schools is completely unacceptable and support schools, teachers, parents and young people to tackle this widespread problem. Our report sets out clear recommendations for how this can be achieved and we hope that the Government will implement them immediately."

A national solution

The Committee urges the Government to act now to protect and empower a generation of children and young people. Key recommendations are:

⇨ The Government must use the new Education Bill to ensure every school takes appropriate action to prevent and respond to sexual harassment and sexual violence. Schools will need support from the Government to achieve this, including clear national guidance.

⇨ Ofsted and the Independent Schools Inspectorate must assess schools on how well they are recording, monitoring, preventing and responding to incidents of sexual harassment and sexual violence.

⇨ Every child at primary and secondary school must have access to high-quality, age-appropriate relationships and sex education delivered by well-trained individuals. This can only be achieved by making sex and relationships education (SRE) a statutory subject; investing in teacher training; and investing in local third sector specialist support.

Girlguiding

Girlguiding's Advocate panel, a group of 14- to 25-year-olds who represent Girlguiding's young members, said:

"As young women, many of us are still in school and experience or witness sexual harassment from groping to cat calling on a daily basis. It's humiliating and frightening and affects what we wear, where we go, our body image and our confidence to speak out in class. Yet, it's often dismissed as 'banter' or a 'compliment' and we are told we are overreacting or being over sensitive.

"It needs to stop. Schools should be safe and empowering places and we should feel able to learn without fear. That's why we need a zero tolerance approach to sexual harassment where schools take the issue seriously, sex and relationship education is compulsory, and schools are held accountable for preventing and tackling sexual harassment.

"It's great the Women and Equalities Committee report is bringing the issue to light and proposing solutions for the Government which will have a big impact on girls' lives."

Teachers' response

Kevin Courtney, National Union of Teachers (NUT) General Secretary said:

"The NUT welcomes the Women and Equalities Committee focus on the issue of sexual harassment and sexual violence in schools. It is an issue that many teachers tell us needs addressing.

"Government education policies hinder schools ability to tackle sexual harassment and sexual bullying effectively by leaving no time for pastoral care or Personal, Social, Health and Economic Education (PSHE) within the curriculum or school day.

"Support and guidance from the Department for Education (DfE) about how to best mitigate the effects of sexual harassment and sexual violence is urgently required. Government needs to provide real leadership on this issue and widen their vision of the purpose of education".

13 September 2016

⇨ The above information is reprinted with kind permission from Parliament UK. Please visit www.parliament.uk for further information.

Reporting sexual offences in schools: an incomplete picture

In brief

Claim

The reports of sexual offences in schools have almost trebled over four years, others say it has more than doubled.

Conclusion

These are correct but the figures are incomplete, so don't show the full picture across the UK.

"Reports of sexual offences in UK schools more than doubled in four years, figures obtained by Plan International UK revealed." *Plan International UK, August 2016*

"School sex crime claims treble in four years, with kids as young as five accused of offences." *The Sun, 7 August 2016*

"The number of sex offences in schools reported to police has almost trebled in four years, a study has shown." *The Guardian, 8 August 2016*

These claims are correct, but the figures they're based on don't show the full picture.

The figures were also reported in a number of other papers including the *Mirror*, the *Daily Mail*, and the *Daily Express* and also on Sky.

The number of sexual offences reported in schools increased from 719 in 2011/12 to 1,955 in 2014/15 according to research obtained by Plan International UK from a number of Freedom of Information requests to UK police forces.

This is more than double, but not quite triple, the numbers from four years ago.

Offences are being reported more, but that doesn't mean they are increasing

The key thing to note about these figures is that they represent reported sexual offences, they can't confirm whether the number of sexual offences in schools is increasing or decreasing. What they show is that more offences are being reported to police.

This could be because more offences are taking place. It could be because people are more aware of the potential for sexual offences to occur in schools and so report them more, due to recent high-profile cases of child abuse or police awareness drives. It could be both.

The point is we just don't know.

The information is incomplete so it's impossible to see the whole picture

The information was gathered from 34 of the 45 police forces across the UK. Police Scotland and a number of other forces did not provide any data and so the figures for all years will be higher than has been reported.

We spoke to Plan International UK and they also said that a number of cases couldn't be allocated to individual years. From 2011/12 to 2014/15 there were 4,711 sexual offences reported to the 34 police forces.

The way crimes are recorded often changes from police force to police force. We found the information provided to Plan International by some of the police forces.

For example, the Metropolitan Police's response notes that their data shouldn't be compared with other forces because of this. West Yorkshire Police say that their information might not cover all sexual offences in schools, because they don't always have to record where the offence took place.

The *Mirror* and *The Guardian* both reported that 29% of reported offenders were pupils and 15% were teachers and other school staff. This is based on figures released by Plan International UK in their press release.

But Plan International also told us that not all of the 34 police forces who responded to them answered all of their questions, so the picture is incomplete.

19 August 2016

⇨ The above information is reprinted with kind permission from Full Fact. Please visit www.fullfact.org for further information.

More than a quarter of a million girls in Britain are unhappy, report reveals

By Amy Packham

More than a quarter of a million girls in Britain are unhappy with their lives, according to the latest *Good Childhood Report*.

The Children's Society's annual review of young people's well-being found an estimated 283,000 girls aged 10–15 are not happy with their lives "overall".

The picture is even starker when it comes to personal appearance, with the number of 10- to 15-year-old girls who do not feel happy with their looks reaching 700,000 across the UK.

"It is desperately worrying that so many of our young people are suffering rather than thriving," said Matthew Reed, Chief Executive of The Children's Society.

"Girls are having a particularly tough time and it's clear that concerted action is needed to tackle this problem."

The report, which is a collaboration between The Children's Society and the University of York, uses evidence from a number of sources, including school and household surveys conducted by the charity.

It referenced one teenage girl who explained why it was so hard being a young person.

"Girls are having a particularly tough time and it's clear that concerted action is needed to tackle this problem"

"There are so many pressures from your friends, from your family," the anonymous girl said. "You don't know who you are going to be, you are trying to find who you are in a certain way."

Another said: "Girls feel pressured by the boys that they should look a particular way and that leads girls into depression or low self-esteem and makes girls feel ugly or worthless."

One teenage girl said: "There is a lot of pressure to look good, you get called names no matter what, people always say stuff behind your back, boys always call you ugly if you have spots, or a slag if you wear makeup."

The concerning part of this report is that the picture for girls is even worse than it was five years previously.

The number of girls who do not feel happy overall was up 21% between 2009/10 and 2013/14. The number of girls unhappy with their appearance in particular was up 8% over the same period.

In contrast, the proportion of boys aged 10–15 who are unhappy with their lives remained stable at one in nine, while the proportion of boys who say they are unhappy with their appearance hovers around 20%.

The trend builds on findings from the 2015 *Good Childhood Report*, in which England ranked last out of 15 countries for happiness with appearance.

The report suggested that emotional bullying such as name-calling, which girls are more likely to experience, is twice as common as physical bullying, which is more likely to affect boys.

About half of all children aged 10–15 had been bullied at school in the past month, the report found.

This year's *Good Childhood Report* highlights the clear link between unhappiness and mental health problems, underlining the importance of tackling low well-being to address mental ill-health.

Boys and girls experience mental health problems in different ways. While boys aged 10 and 11 are less happy than girls with their school work and more likely to experience conduct and attention/hyperactivity problems, girls experience anxiety and depression significantly more than boys – and become increasingly unhappy with their appearance – as they get older.

"Social media... has been linked to a higher risk of mental ill-health"

Separate research by the Office for National Statistics suggests that girls are much more likely to spend extended periods on social media, which has been linked to a higher risk of mental ill-health.

Social media has been linked to poor self-esteem and mental health issues in the past.

An exclusive poll for HuffPost UK's Young Minds Matter series earlier this year, guest edited by The Duchess of Cambridge, of parents found four-fifths (81%) of those surveyed blame social media for making their children more vulnerable to mental health problems.

The Children's Society is calling on Government to take action to improve children's happiness across the nation with a legal entitlement for children to be able to access mental health and wellbeing support in schools and FE colleges across England and Wales.

"All children deserve a happy childhood and we must never accept that it is somehow inevitable that so many children in Britain should live in distress," added Reed.

"As a first step all children should be able to access mental health and wellbeing support in school.

"Children must be heard and helped."

31 August 2016

⇨ The above information is reprinted with kind permission from The Huffington Post UK. Please visit www.huffingtonpost.co.uk for further information.

No, you're not "hardwired" to stare at women's breasts

THE CONVERSATION

An article from The Conversation.

By Michelle Smith, Research fellow in English Literature, Deakin University

You'll likely know by now about the Free the Nipple Picnic event held in Brisbane on 17 January, described by one of its organisers as:

"Just a way for us to sit around in an open public area and feel that we can have our nipples free and have great discussions."

The *Free the Nipple* campaign – named after Lina Esco's 2014 film – is a global push to desexualise women's breasts and allow women the freedom to be topless in the same places in which it is acceptable for men and boys to do so. But are such campaigns ridiculous in a hypersexualised porn culture? Isn't the sexual appeal of breasts for men, and many women, "hardwired" and unable to be changed?

The Brisbane picnic drew the attention of hundreds of men online who were troubled that men were excluded from attending, even though the event was intended to provide a safe space for women to gather, free from "sexualisation".

Contemporary Western culture codes breasts as erotic objects, as the increasing practice of breast enlargement through implants illustrates.

Much of the discomfort and shaming surrounding public breastfeeding stems from the overwhelming understanding of breasts as sexually arousing to the viewer.

There have been repeated instances in which Facebook, for example, has deleted photographs of mothers breastfeeding.

The site's most recent nudity policy restricts "some images of female breasts if they include the nipple" but now allows "photos of women actively engaged in breastfeeding".

What is often overlooked in discussions about the sexual appeal of breasts is the fact that they have not always been regarded as irresistibly attractive in all points in history and across all cultures.

Other parts of women's bodies have been viewed as more enticing than breasts, including buttocks, legs, ankles, hair and feet. Bound feet (or the "golden lotus") in ancient China had strong erotic connections and acts that could be performed with them were detailed in illustrated sex manuals.

Some of these body parts have no connection to a woman's capacity to reproduce or nurture her offspring, as is often suggested to explain the modern fixation on large breasts. (Greater breast size, or more fatty tissue, does not mean that a woman can produce more milk than a smaller breasted woman.)

Buttocks are actually a greater marker of a woman's fertility than breasts. Buttocks show whether women have sufficient stores of fat to sustain a pregnancy, signal pelvic size and are prominent when young, becoming less pronounced with age.

The appeal of larger buttocks is evident in historical fashion trends such as the bustle in the 19th century, but also among certain racial groups in modern culture. African-American and Hispanic communities are the most likely to seek out buttock augmentation (implants), and hip hop music has given us dozens of odes to large "booties".

The body parts that different cultures fetishise are often those that must be covered by clothing. In the words of author Elizabeth Wilson, in her 1985 book *Adorned in Dreams: Fashion and Modernity*:

"Even in societies whose members ordinarily wear few clothes, it is said to be customary to dress up for dancing ceremonies and other occasions on which sexual interest is likely to be aroused. It is often said that dress enhances sexual attraction because it both reveals and conceals the body."

Breasts are an example of concealment feeding into sexual attraction today, but there are other instances that reveal how this process is not the result of an innate, "hardwired" desire.

Buttocks and breasts might be sexualised, in part, because of their proximity to genitalia and status as secondary sexual characteristics, but how can the eroticisation of women's ankles be explained?

In Victorian Britain, respectable women wore long skirts and dresses that covered the entirety of their legs. As the author Jane Nicholas put it in *The Modern Girl* (2015), the fact that these areas were always concealed meant that "a glimpse of an ankle or calf could be erotic" for men.

Like ankles, head hair has no inherent sexual function, but it has also been eroticised within numerous religious traditions that have, in turn, required women to keep their hair veiled. Many Muslim girls and women cover their hair outside the home, and in some Jewish communities married women wear hats, scarves or wigs to hide their own hair from view.

These taboos on the exposure of women's ankles and hair in public illustrate that the parts of women's bodies that are considered sexually arousing are changeable in different times and places and that concealing them only adds to their forbidden allure.

When thinking about the *Free the Nipple* movement, there is also the obvious point that many traditional cultures around the world did not require women to cover their breasts until the intervention of Christian missionaries or introduction of Islam. In locations where women are routinely topless, attitudes towards breasts are, unsurprisingly, different to places in which there are prohibitions on their exposure.

None of this is to deny that many people derive pleasure from looking at breasts or that women themselves often derive sensual pleasure from their breasts. But when it comes to the debate about whether women should be able to appear in public topless, we can challenge the idea that an unstoppable desire to gaze on women's breasts in a sexual way is an inherent part of male biological makeup that will never alter.

Just as we might not understand why a Victorian woman could not stride down the street with her calves exposed, so too might we look back in future with some mystification at the idea that a few topless women having a picnic could provoke heated debate.

31 January 2016

⇨ The above information is reprinted with kind permission from *The Conversation*. Please visit www.theconversation.com for further information.

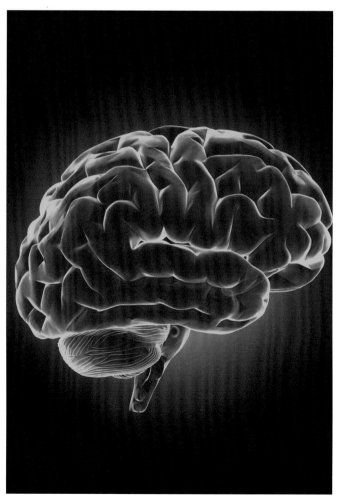

From Jane Fonda to bikini body children's classes, why do we sex up female fitness?

By Celia Walden

How would you feel if your 11-year-old daughter signed up for "bikini body" fitness classes? It's that time of year, after all, we're being told to get "beach ready" (another cretinous term) – and much as you'd like to keep her in that burkini until her mid-to-late thirties, she's going to be a little lady soon.

A little lady with body image issues, if the Ripley Academy in Derbyshire – who caused outrage last week after advertising the class – has anything to do with it. Actually that's more than a little unfair. Once the furore blew up, in the way that only a news story involving schoolgirls and anything to do with sex in the age of social media can, it was quickly made clear that the school's principal, Carey Ayres, had been unaware of the wording used on posters advertising the after-school class – which had been written without permission by an over-zealous supply teacher (presumably hopped up on the weekly women's magazine zeitgeist).

The school has since apologised and assured its parents that "we would never condone any class, or after-school activity, that may put pressure on any young person in terms of their own body image". No harm, no foul. But it was the words of a concerned parent that stayed with me: "This is sexualising the fitness class." To which – if I were in the habit of calling people 'honey' – I would say: "Honey, that ship has sailed."

Why? Because what is deeply unacceptable for girls of 11–18 remains unacceptable for grown women. And 36 years after the world fitness craze first exploded at the start of the 80s, the sexualisation of female exercise continues – only in a far more insidious fashion. We all look back with indulgence at Jane Fonda's first fitness video, released in 1982 – to be enjoyed by men and women in very different ways. Likewise, Cindy Crawford's early Noughties offering – a sort of Fifty Shades-style work-out in which the panting supermodel gets twisted into knots on a Manhattan rooftop by a trainer/sadomasochistic master named 'Radu' – may have been criticised for having a far more beneficial effect on the male anatomy than the female, but was basically passed off as light entertainment.

Now, despite well-meaning campaigns like "This Girl Can" – aimed to get women and girls moving any way they can without fear of judgement – and a conscious effort on behalf of parts of the fitness industry to promote health, strength and power over bikini body idealism, physical exercise is still being sold to women with the promise of sexual appeal. "Picture yourself rockin' that LBD!" the spandex-clad she-bot I pay 20 bucks to torture me in LA likes to holler. 50 minutes into an hour-long spin class, even the stragglers at the back will pick up the pace here: that's the power of visualisation for you (and yet curiously "picture the blood flow promoting the growth of new brain cells in your hippocampus" doesn't quite do it). But instead of surging towards the heady image of myself in that little black dress, I always slow down – and glance at the men. "Aren't you going to get these guys to picture themselves in a pair of thigh skimming XXS Vilebrequins?" I'll wonder. But the she-bot never does.

Because whereas women have got to really sweat it out – sculpt, tauten and lengthen those limbs – in order find or keep a mate, men will get the girl whatever they look like. That's the implication, isn't it?

It should be laughable, and it would be if the sexualisation of fitness didn't put off precisely the women who need to get moving most. "It's the idea of having to put on all that revealing gear," one of my closest friends – anxious to lose her baby weight – complained. And when you look at the Rihanna-inspired cutaway, mesh and fishnet creations being touted as yoga or exercise gear – and worn by the likes of Kim Kardashian as daywear to demonstrate sexual desirability – it's no wonder many women can't get past that first stumbling block. Who wants to be doing 'burpees' in something you'd buy from Ann Summers? Not me.

Which is why, despite having been a fitness freak for 20 years, I've always refused to invest in the faddish accoutrements the industry tries to bully us all into buying, just as I've always refused to invest in the notion that running, swimming or spinning will make me any prettier, sexier or bikini-body readier. I'll settle for it making me feel good.

20 May 2016

'Come on Rude Boy': the sexualisation of modern music

By Bruno Russell

In the last decade or so, music has become increasingly sexualised. From Rihanna asking the 'Rude Boy' to step up, Ariana Grande asking to 'Let Me Love You' and Nicki Minaj saying her "Anaconda don't want none unless you've got buns hun", we can't escape the sexual advances in modern day pop culture. But what really is so problematic about this increasing sexualisation?

It would seem that these powerful sexual advances are driven by female empowerment: women assert their own sexuality and take control of the power-play in the bedroom. But is it really having this effect? Recent research, conducted by Dr Justin Coulson, found that in reality, "These female artists are selling the message that women are nothing more than accessories. Women are only of value as sexual objects. My daughters and your daughters are taught to conform to this narrow sexualised, unhealthy norm." Essentially, women are becoming the sexual objects of men.

When Rihanna, therefore, declares that 'Bitch Better Have My Money'

she does little to declare female power, and more to enhance sexual stereotypes that leave men feeling they have the upper hand. Due to the influential power of music, this is extremely damaging; this image inevitably becomes ingrained in society's psych. Of course, not only women sexualise themselves in their music. We all recall the famous 'Blurred Lines' lyrics and video stereotyping male fascination in the female body. But this stereotypes men as the sexual predator and they are very rarely shown as being submissive to women. Thus seeming to only reinforce the notion of men having the upper hand. Of course there are other knock-on effects: this type of male sexualisation likely shapes and moulds societal ideas of masculinity that then affect men who do not adhere to it. 'Camp' men can therefore feel isolated from the male community because of its obsession with linking the 'hard' man obsessed with women to some kind of 'proper' masculinity. Perhaps this helps explain why 'camp' men often favour female artists, and gay clubs play

more female music than male music; stressing this norm. It's some kind of musical revolt but one that in reality is only acting within the stereotype boundaries (and could, potentially, be part of the reason the gay male community is more likely to have the epithet 'slut' assigned them than the straight male community).

A more central problem, however, is that an increased number of male-orientated music sexualises women in a derogatory way and gets away with it under the guise of creativity. 'Smack That' by Akon and 'Loyal' by Chris Brown are perfect examples of songs that portray women as the sexual play thing, but somehow pass as acceptable in current society – and indeed are promoted and danced along to by men and women alike – because it's music, it's an 'art'. But what this does is subconsciously enforce a view in the male community that this type of behaviour is OK when projected into reality, not helped by the rising trend of male domination in the bedroom (as a form of BDSM) which is perhaps itself a result of the increased exploration of sexuality in our everyday music. Even women sometimes reinforce this, if we cast our mind back to Christina Aguilera's 'Your Body' where men "don't need no key, I'm unlocked… and I won't tell you to stop". It's creating this picture that women are 'easy' and the play thing of men. Of course, many women rightfully stand against this image, but why then do we allow music to hold this view and express it in contemporary society. Surely we are shooting ourselves in the foot?

Research, conducted by the American Psychological Association, also links sexualisation to eating disorders, low self-esteem and depression. This shows that this type of sexualisation is not only damaging in terms of enforcing gender stereotypes, but is actually affecting people's physical and mental well-being. Women feel they have to be thin and look

Action to protect children from viewing age-inappropriate music videos online

Further action is being taken to protect children from viewing inappropriate music videos on the internet.

- Government and major UK music labels agree to make successful pilot programme permanent.

- Clear age ratings now displayed by Vevo and YouTube on UK-produced music videos that are not suitable for children.

- Further work underway with digital service providers to explore how parental controls could be applied to music videos.

The Government is working with the UK music industry, BBFC and digital service providers like Vevo and YouTube to take further action to protect children from viewing inappropriate videos on the internet.

Many children have easy access to music videos online and some parents are rightly concerned that some of these contain imagery or lyrics not appropriate for a young audience.

In October 2014 a Government-backed pilot to introduce age ratings for online music videos was launched by the BBFC and BPI in conjunction with Vevo and YouTube, working with major UK music labels to introduce a new ratings system that would allow digital service providers to clearly display an easily recognisable age rating on videos posted on the web.

UK labels supply videos ahead of release to the BBFC, and then pass on the rating and guidance given by the BBFC when releasing their videos to the two digital service providers involved – Vevo and YouTube - who display it when the videos are broadcast online.

Building on the pilot, the Government has now as part of its manifesto commitment agreed with the UK music industry and with the digital service providers that the measures trialled will be now be made permanent for videos produced in the UK by artists who are represented by major labels.

As well as working with Sony Music UK, Universal Music UK and Warner Music UK, the Government is also encouraging independent UK music labels to follow suit so that the digital service providers can display appropriate age ratings on their videos too. We can announce today that independent UK music labels will now take part in a six month pilot phase.

18 August 2015

- Department for Culture, Media & Sport and Baroness Joanna Shields. GOV.UK.

---

like Ariana Grande otherwise they are 'lesser' and not alluring to men, leaving them prone to anorexic-type illnesses. Equally, if they fail to "live up" to this image set by music they then can feel depressed or uncomfortable in expressing their sexuality. Music teaches us that women have to be sexy for men to be 'Into You'.

The other reason for this increased sexualisation is that sex sells! The recent most popular club and chart music – making thousands of pounds – has become known for its ability to be slut dropped or twerked along too. Thus the likes of Fifth Harmony, Beyoncé, Pitbull and Flo Ride fill our clubs and make us lower our hips. This also then reflects a more recent youth culture than enjoys a more flexibly lax attitude to sexuality through dancing than previous generations have allowed. This type of music is, in some ways, the modern generations stand against the sexual constraint of previous generations, which is put

on us as children. It's us declaring our sexuality. This, it all seems, is a good thing (depending on your views on the current attitude to sex amongst youngsters). The point is that this can be done in a healthy way: Fifth Harmony manage to create 'slutty' music without needing to objectify women as sexual objects or refer to explicit sexual references (think 'Work from Home' or 'All in My Head'). Rihanna, and similar artists, however, cannot, and rely on sexual imagery (think the lap dancer imagine of 'Pour It Up') to create this idea. Perhaps we can have sexualisation in music by its beats without needing explicitly objectifying lyrics?

What then do we do? Whilst we all enjoy dancing along to these slutty songs in clubs, it seems the modern sexualisation in pop music is having grave effects on both gender stereotyping and our own well-being. Is this really worth the sacrifice of enjoying music? Is it possible to

sustain modern music removing this sexualisation (surely that's what the likes of Adele achieves)? There seems to be little danger in sexual dancing, indeed if an expression of sexuality I would promote it, but can we have this without then having these worrying negative repercussions?

This is all left to be seen. But at the moment we can say that there is a problem, and it seems something needs to be done about it before it gets completely out of hand.

25 August 2016

⇨ The above information is reprinted with kind permission from *The Edge*. Please visit www. theedgesusu.co.uk for further information.

Beyonce's 'bootylicious' sexualisation of black women isn't inspiring – and her politics leave a lot to be desired

The Black Panthers were a Marxist revolutionary organisation who believed capitalism would always oppress black communities. They would have balked at their image being used at the Super Bowl.

By Kehinde Andrews

For days now there has been praise (and condemnation) pouring out for Beyonce's Super Bowl half-time show performance and her boldness in making statements on race on such a mainstream stage.

"The scantily clad, booty-shaking salute to the Panthers from Beyonce sadly played into many of those ideas of a woman's place as 'decoration' in the struggle"

After all, it is rare to see Black Power salutes and artists singing how they love their 'negro nose' on such a platform. However, I have to confess that I watched the half-time show and almost missed the political stance entirely, wrapped as it was in the "bootylicious" over-sexualisation of black women that we have come to expect from Beyonce.

Never before has so much been made over a one-and-a-half-minute performance, with everyone so quick to embrace a performance that was the epitome of style over substance.

In October it will be 50 years since the formation of the Black Panther Party for Self Defense by Huey P Newton and Bobby Seale in Oakland, California. This is an important anniversary to mark because the Panthers provided a radical alternative to the politics of mainstream acceptance.

In fact, the Panthers were a Marxist revolutionary organisation who believed that capitalism would always oppress black communities. There are few less appropriate venues to pay homage to the party than in the pinnacle of consumerism that is the Super Bowl.

The role of women in the Panthers has also often been glossed over, with a focus on the armed 'brothers from the block' who engaged in battles with the police. The Panthers also received many accusations of sexism, made worse when Kwame Ture (then Stokely Carmichael) was quoted as saying that the only place for women in the movement was "prone".

The scantily clad, booty-shaking salute to the Panthers from Beyonce sadly played into many of those ideas of a woman's place as 'decoration' in the struggle. In truth, women were a central part of all of the Panthers' work, including armed defence, the community programmes and leadership.

Part of the reason for the amount of praise for the performance is because this is not something people expected from Beyonce. In the past she has received a lot of criticism for her lack of politics and her perceived negative representation of black women, in particular after she faced accusation of skin lightening for promotional purposes, which were strongly denied.

We are in an era where mainstream artists are keen to protect their brands and not to alienate white audiences. This has not always been the case, however, and there is a long history in both the US and the UK of black artists playing a key role in political movements. The best example, with regards to Beyonce, would be Aretha Franklin, who publicly supported the Panthers by providing bail money in the high-profile case of Angela Davis.

It speaks volumes that Beyonce has caused such a stir from a symbolic gesture, but I fear that this 'quick click' generation is getting the shallow politics we deserve.

The issues that face black communities worldwide are serious and entrenched. #BlackLivesMatter has called attention to some of the worst abuses of police power in the US, but these represent the tip of the iceberg in regards to deeply rooted racial inequalities. It is not enough to try to find pride and comfort in symbolic gestures; we need to work to rebuild organisations and politics of resistance.

"The test of Beyonce's politics will be what she does now, because one half time show performance does not make a revolution"

With their considerable wealth and appeal, Beyonce and her husband Jay Z – who were once reported to have bailed out #BlackLivesMatter protesters themselves – could play a major role in developing a politics of resistance.

However, the test of Beyonce's politics will be what she does now, because one half-time show performance does not make a revolution.

11 February 2016

⇨ The above information is reprinted with kind permission from *The Independent*. Please visit www.independent.co.uk for further information.

Over one quarter of males agree that men are sexualised in adverts just as much as women

It seems that the rise of 'Hunkvertising' is causing men to avert their eyes away from advertising. Indeed, new research from market intelligence agency Mintel reveals that half (50%) of all men say they don't pay much attention to advertising, whilst more than one quarter (26%) agree that men are sexualised in adverts just as much as women are.

Mintel research indicates that advertising is making young males feel inadequate about their appearance, as one in six (17%) men aged 16–24 agree that male models in advertising have made them more self-conscious of their looks, up from an average of 11%. Older men, meanwhile, may feel marginalised, with 70% of men aged over 65 agreeing they don't pay attention to advertising.

Today, just 8% of men say they are inspired by the way men look in advertising, and it seems many feel alienated by the way their gender is currently portrayed. One quarter (25%) say they find it hard to identify with men that are shown in adverts, whilst 22% say that men are too stereotyped in adverts. Furthermore, one in five (20%) agree that advertising too often portrays men as incompetent in the home.

Jack Duckett, Consumer Lifestyles Analyst at Mintel, said:

"The trend for using hyper-athletic male models and celebrities in advertising has grown significantly in recent years, giving rise to the term 'Hunkvertising', and resulting in men today being just as sexualised in advertising campaigns as women. Whilst this holds a level of aspiration for some men, for many more it has resulted in feelings of inadequacy. This points to an opportunity for brands to create more campaigns that feature average, everyday men."

As well as driving men away from advertising, it seems the unrealistic body image portrayed in advertising is having an effect on men's lifestyle priorities. Today, Mintel research shows that men are more likely to list being in good shape as a future priority than they are to list having a relationship. Almost half (45%) of men say that being in good shape is a priority for the future, compared to 38% who prioritise getting married or being in a long-term relationship, followed by having children (23%) and being promoted at work (18%).

Furthermore, men aged 16 to 34 rank being in good shape above having a close group of friends as half (50%) of this say that being in good shape is currently a priority compared to 44% who prioritise having and maintaining a close group of friends. What's more, being in good shape trumps healthy eating amongst this age group, as just 48% of men aged 16–34 say this is a current priority.

"Health has been a dominant trend in the UK in recent years, and this is evidenced by the high proportion of men who cite eating healthily and being in good shape both as current and future priorities. With advertising increasingly promoting hyper-athletic bodies as a symbol of modern masculinity, men are feeling under pressure to emulate the physiques they see on screen". Jack comments.

But it seems that it is not just their physique which men are image-conscious over. When shopping for clothing, shoes and accessories, one in five (19%) men say it's important to purchase a well-known brand compared to 16% of women. Indeed, price is less important to male consumers, as 66% of women say it's important to buy clothes that are good value for money compared to 55% of men. What's more, 47% of women say it's important that these products are on sale or on offer, compared to less than two in five (38%) men.

Finally, it is not just male models which men are growing averse to, as 30% of men find adverts featuring female models clichéd, while 26% deem these sexist and another 15% find them patronising.

"Men's brands can play a bigger role in the push for gender equality, helping to garner favour with male consumers who already champion equality, as well as helping to educate others about its value," Jack concludes.

27 January 2016

⇨ The above information is reprinted with kind permission from Mintel. Please visit www.mintel.com for further information.

Let's talk about sexualisation in video games

By James Batchelor

With the line between what players find acceptable and offensive seemingly blurring, James Batchelor asks how developers can ensure they design characters without controversy

It's no secret: sex sells. But there's a difference between creating appealing, marketable characters and oversexualising them to the point of gratuitousness.

The problem is, the line between them is increasingly hard to define. Online debates around characters in *Overwatch*, *Street Fighter*, *Metal Gear Solid* and more show conflicting views of what does and doesn't need to be censored.

In this climate, designing a heroine for your game might seem a risky business, so how do you ensure you avoid offending your audience?

First, says Rhianna Pratchett – the writer behind the *Tomb Raider* reboot – we need to establish the difference between "sexualised" and "sexy".

"Sexualisation is not inherently a bad thing," she says. "Context is the key. For me, 'sexy' is based on the character, while 'sexualised' is about the audience.

"Sexy is more than just looks – it's about attitude, personality and a certain amount of owned power. Sexy transcends gender, age and sexual orientation. Meanwhile, sexualisation tends to be about the perceived desires of an audience. And characters can be both. Take Bayonetta, for example: she is definitely sexualised, but at the same time owns her sexuality. It's very much part of who she is, she is in control and that's sexy as hell."

TV host, writer and producer Liana Kerzner adds: "I'd love developers to start rethinking what it means to be a sexy woman. In the real world, people find women sexy for being intelligent, competent and tough – a dress that defies physics isn't a requirement."

The way you look

Much of the debate comes down to visual design – and a lack of realism.

"Observe the proportions of real women and strive to create female characters who represent a more normative look that would resonate with the majority of women," advises IGDA executive director Kate Edwards.

"Recent games such as *Mirror's Edge* and the *Tomb Raider* reboot have done a better job of creating female characters who look more natural, and their appearance and lack of extreme proportions don't detract from the gameplay or story in any way."

This also applies to your characters' wardrobes – specifically the practicality of what they are wearing.

"You can tell a lot of male designers don't know the first thing about how women's clothing works, because they put all this practical detail into their male characters' armour, then create female wardrobes that are stupid," says Kerzner.

"Take Cammy from *Street Fighter*. Her costume is strong, cute and sexy all at once – but any woman who has done gymnastics or martial arts will tell you a bodysuit with no legs ends up riding up your butt."

Animation is another oft-criticised aspect of female characters, with many arguing that walking with an exaggerated hip swing is overly sexualised. A recent episode of Anita Sarkeesian's *Tropes vs Women In Video Games* series was almost entirely dedicated to the difference between male and female animations.

> ## "Sexualisation is not inherently a bad thing. Context is the key. For me, 'sexy' is based on the character, while 'sexualised' is about the audience"
>
> *Rhianna Pratchett*

"Realistic bodies should move like bodies," says Kerzner. "Natural breasts move very differently than implants, and a lot of boobs in video games move –

or don't move – like they were installed by a surgeon. When you make a female character look like she's had implants put in, that's a character trait. It's something that should be decided more consciously than it currently is."

Kerzner adds that even voice acting needs to be considered if you're trying to portray a realistic female character: "Real women get angry, yell, swear and throw things. Take the limiter off. Female characters are shackled because developers are too worried about them being 'likeable'.

"I've done voicework, and I'm always astounded that the directors tend to select the most vanilla take I give them. Accents, interesting inflections, and anything that would add character to the character tend to be passed over for dialogue delivery that's inoffensive above all else. I've gotten really good at what I call the 'Disney Princess voice', because it's the only thing that's currently considered safe. As a performer, though, it's really damned boring."

Pratchett says the secret to creating a balanced character is to consider every aspect of them carefully, and question the choices you are making.

"Don't overemphasise the sexuality or gender of a character, either through their art, animation or narrative," she suggests. "And, in the words of Mr Timberlake, bring sexy back. Build a character's sexuality into who they are, not who you want them to be for. Ask yourself: who is this character, how do they act, dress, talk, and why? Don't just stuff them into a skimpy outfit and think 'job done' – unless your game is basically about stuffing characters into skimpy outfits, of course.

"If you're trying to hit a wider demographic – and the audience for games is more diverse than it ever has been before – why wouldn't you just pay more attention to your characters? Make them more than just their gender, sexuality or looks. Appeal to your audience through the myriad of human emotions and responses. Not just what makes them hot. And if your game is about making players hot – because VR porn games are coming, right? – then own it."

Talking about tracer

A recent example of the debate around sexualised game characters centred on Blizzard's latest release *Overwatch*.

Originally the Tracer character was shown in the pose you can see here, but the studio changed it after complaints that this was not in keeping with her character. We asked our experts for their thoughts.

Rhianna Pratchett says: "Although I didn't personally find Tracer's pose a big deal, I did think it was interesting that many people – including the developers themselves – seemed to feel that the sexualised pose just didn't fit with her character.

"However, very little fuss was made about a character like Widowmaker, who is more traditionally sexualised, because it had been built into her character and was part of who she was. Context matters."

Liana Kerzner believes there are far worse examples out there: "I didn't even think she was that sexualised – she just had a wedgie. The *Overwatch* character designs, across the board, are astoundingly good, and they're all sexy in their own way. Tracer is a character who I think has a crazy sexy voice. And yet someone determined that it's wrong for her to ever be conventionally sexy, because... 'think of the children'."

Real women

Kerzner observes that there's a distinct difference in how many male and female characters are presented. Men, she says, often tend to be relatable, while women are 'perfected'.

"This double standard needs to change," she says. "If you choose realism, any romanticised element will seem out of place. But developers constantly design realistic men and romantic women in the same game.

"Real female cops, firefighters, army veterans and MMA fighters have a steel to their appearance that we don't see in the current crop of 'likeable' heroines. There are exceptions: Anna Grimsdottir in *Splinter Cell*, for instance. She looks like she's had late nights, stress and too much coffee. She's still glamorous and sexy, but she doesn't still have the skin tone

of a 16-year-old. Similarly, Jayma in *Far Cry Primal* is covered in scars from animal attacks because she's a hunter."

"We've been indoctrinated with the idea that games are inherently made for a 'presumed male audience', and while that's true for some games, it's not across the board"

Liana Kerzner

Female characters are often cited as overly sexualised, but our experts argue this happens to men as well – yet people aren't talking about it.

"We see many male characters that are unnatural in appearance, with perfectly chiselled bodies and rippling muscles," Edwards says. "The difference is that many of these male characters are viewed as powerful and strong, whereas the appearance of most female characters skews more towards sex appeal."

Kerzner agrees, adding: "Catwoman from the Arkham games has been criticised for the way she walks, having a sexy voice and so on. But what about the hyper-masculine Batman?

"He is depicted with the physique of a bodybuilder even though his combat style is martial arts. His heavy boots would negatively impact his ability to climb buildings.

"Why was Catwoman singled out for criticism? Because we criticise a woman for being overtly sexy in ways we don't criticise men."

The debate continues

While fresh examples crop up all the time, this is not a new discussion – nor is it confined to our own industry. As Pratchett observes: "All entertainment fields, particularly comics, are discussing this topic in some form or another."

But it is something the games industry should be more conscious of – especially given the gender 'balance' of our global workforce. A 2015 IGDA survey discovered that 79 per cent of developers are male.

"This means we're more likely to see representations that appeal to the male eye," says Edwards. "This is slowly changing as more developers realise

that oversexualised character design is becoming passé and unnecessary for serving the intent of most games.

"We see many male characters that are unnatural in appearance, with perfectly chiselled bodies and rippling muscles. The difference is these are viewed as powerful and strong, whereas the appearance of most female characters skews more towards sex appeal"

Kate Edwards, IGDA

"Ultimately, the artistic freedom of game developers needs to be upheld, but developers need to be mindful of their creative choices, especially if their intent is to maximise their game's appeal across all demographics."

Kerzner concludes: "We've been indoctrinated with the idea that games are inherently made for a 'presumed male audience', and while that's true for some games, it's not across the board. Look at the early marketing for the Atari 2600 and the NES: the target audience is families.

"The problem is TV marketing, which is subject to rigid filtering by target audience, and gaming content for women is seen as 'too niche'. Gaming is stuck between a rock and a hard place: its marketing doesn't match its products. The industry's growth with women is being restricted by unnatural barriers, and when people get trapped in unnaturally close quarters, they fight. That's what's happening now."

1 June 2016

⇨ The above information is reprinted with kind permission from *Develop*, originally published in the June 2016 edition. Please visit www.develop-online.net for further information.

Black female *Iron Man* cover pulled due to over-sexualisation

Fans accuse – comic book criticised Marvel's depiction of 15-year-old heroine Riri Williams.

Comic book giants Marvel and Midtown Comics have been forced to scrap the specialist cover of the new *Iron Man*, which features long-awaited black heroine Riri Williams, after fans criticised the illustration for over-sexualising the teenager.

The Invincible Iron Man #1 artwork, created by J Scott Campbell, has subsequently been dropped after fans expressed disappointment that the superhero appeared several shades lighter than her original complexion and was drawn with a noticeably mature body.

Teresa Jusino, an assistant editor for The Mary Sue, slammed the cover saying: "It's as though they decided a teenage girl's face was fine," she wrote, "but let's attach a more grown-up body to that face, because she's not a true female superhero until you can imagine having sex with her."

"Fans criticised the illustration for over-sexualising the teenager"

A preview of the originally intended cover was unveiled last week (19 Oct) only to be dropped the day after following the public backlash.

"The writer of the series, Brian Michael Bendis, said that he's glad that Marvel pulled the cover"

Hitting back at criticisms, Campbell defended his artwork on Twitter: "Hmmm. This is the character I was asked to draw, people understand that, right? Is it THAT different?"

"I gave her a sassy 'attitude'," he told one Twitter user. "'Sexualising' was not intended. This reaction is odd. The crop-top was in the existing design."

However, the writer of the series, Brian Michael Bendis, said that he's glad that Marvel pulled the cover.

"Speciality covers are not in my purview and it was being produced separately from the work of the people involved in making the comic," he wrote on Tumblr. "Not to pass the buck but that's the fact. If I had seen a sketch or something I would have voiced similar concerns. I am certain the next version will be amazing."

Williams was announced in July as the successor to the Iron Man legacy laid by billionaire weapons inventor Tony Stark.

She's described as a Chicago-born teenager and genius student who enrolled at the famous technology university MIT, years before her time.

25 October 2016

⇨ The above information is reprinted with kind permission from Voice Online. Please visit www.voice-online.co.uk for further information.

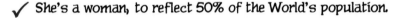
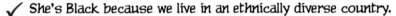

✓ She's a woman, to reflect 50% of the World's population.

✓ She's Black because we live in an ethnically diverse country.

✓ She's sexy to appeal to a big part of our audience: horny teenage males.

The character design committee

Adult magazines in shops

By John Woodhouse and Philip Ward

Summary

The availability of 'soft' pornography and 'men's lifestyle' magazines in newsagents and shops has been criticised as these titles are often on display where they can be seen by children.

What do the guidelines say?

Top-shelf material

Guidelines issued by the National Federation of Retail Newsagents (NFRN) advise that 'soft' pornography should be placed on the top shelf of newsagents.

Other material

The NFRN guidelines recommend that 'men's lifestyle' magazines – sometimes referred to as 'lads' mags' – should not be displayed next to children's titles or at eye-level or below. If this is not possible – e.g. where there is limited display space – the NFRN says that front covers can be part-overlapped with other titles to minimise offence to parents.

Guidance issued by the Association of Convenience Stores makes similar recommendations. It also suggests the use of 'modesty boards'.

1. 'Top-shelf' magazines

National Federation of Retail Newsagents guidelines

There is a voluntary code, operated by newsagents, whereby adult "soft" pornography is placed on the top shelves in shops, out of the reach of children.

The code is operated by the National Federation of Retail Newsagents (NFRN) and applies to titles that publishers categorise as "top shelf" rather than to any title by name. The guidelines (dated November 2014) state:

Adult top-shelf titles:

⇨ Adult Titles should be displayed on the Top Shelf only and out of the reach of children.

⇨ Adult Titles should not be sold to any person under the age of 18 years.

⇨ Adult Titles should only be acquired from bona fide trade channels (on the basis that these will have been vetted by the suppliers' lawyers for compliance with legislation).

⇨ Care and sensitivity should be exercised over the display of Adult Titles with explicit front covers

Members are also advised to be responsive to the views of their customers and, in particular they are advised that they are not obliged to stock these titles if they have objections on religious, moral or other grounds.

The Indecent Displays (Control) Act 1981

As far as the external appearance of 'top shelf' publications is concerned, the relevant legislation is the Indecent Displays (Control) Act 1981. This makes it an offence to display 'indecent matter' in, or so as to be visible in, a public place – the cover of a magazine, rather than its contents, is therefore what matters for the purpose of the Act.

'Indecency' is not statutorily defined, but the degree of offensiveness of indecent material is lower than that of material which risks being obscene under the Obscene Publications Act 1959 (i.e. "having a tendency to deprave and corrupt"). It is possible, therefore, that a publisher who wants to put a particularly explicit cover on a magazine could wrap it in order to avoid prosecution under the 1981 Act.

Alternatively, the publisher could make it available only through a licensed sex shop to which only persons aged 18 or over have access under the Local Government (Miscellaneous Provisions) Act 1982 and which is not therefore a public place.

2. 'Men's lifestyle' magazines

NFRN guidelines for display

The NFRN guidelines also make a number of recommendations for the display of 'men's lifestyle' magazines, often referred to as 'lads' mags':

Men's Lifestyle Magazines (Lads' Mags) with front covers that may offend some customers

Although these are not top-shelf titles, we do urge members to be sensitive to the concerns of consumers, particularly in relation to the display of titles with front covers and/or content that may be inappropriate to display at a young person's eye level or below.

To minimise complaints from consumers, without adversely affecting the sale of these titles, we recommend:

⇨ Do not display them adjacent to your display of children's titles and comics.

⇨ Do not display them at, or below, children's eye level to ensure that they are not in the direct sight and reach of children.

⇨ Part-overlap potentially problematic front covers with other titles to minimise offence to parents where your display space precludes the above suggestions.

⇨ That similar care and consideration is given to the display of any Point of Sale material for these titles.

⇨ A free, industry-agreed planogram indicating the preferred placement of titles is available to download. For further information please visit www.ppa.co.uk/retail.

Association of Convenience Stores guidance

The Association of Convenience Stores (ACS) has also published guidance (2013) on how to display 'men's lifestyle' magazines.[1]

---

1 Available from this section of the ACS website: https://www.acs.org.uk/advice/ladsmags/

This includes the following advice for retailers:

⇨ Ensure that lad's mags are placed on shelf away from any children's titles...

⇨ In stores with smaller units, where moving the product out of the eye line of children is not possible, you can part obscure the titles with other magazines to ensure potentially offensive images can't be seen.

⇨ You may decide that none of the above options are practical or sufficient to meet your customers concerns. In this case you should consider the use of modesty boards.

'Lose the Lads' Mags' campaign

In 2013, UK Feminista[2] and Object[3] coordinated a 'Lose the Lads' Mags' campaign. This called for supermarkets and newsagents to stop selling the magazines, claiming they portrayed women as "dehumanised sex objects".[4]

Some commentators argued that lads' mags were an easy target and that 'gossip' magazines also objectified and portrayed women in demeaning ways but were not the subject of any campaigns.[5]

In July 2013, the Co-op said that it would no longer sell lad's mags unless they were supplied in sealed modesty bags to prevent children seeing "overtly sexual images".[6] In September 2013, the Co-op announced that it would no longer sell *Nuts*, *Zoo*, *Front*, or the midweek and *Sunday Sport* newspapers.[7]

Nuts, *FHM*, *Loaded* and *Zoo* have

2 A group campaigning for gender equality: http://ukfeminista.org.uk/about/

3 A group campaigning "for better representation of women & girls in the media & against sex object culture": http://objectupdate. tumblr.com/

4 Ibid

5 "Even lads' mags aren't as bad as the gossip rags", *Telegraph*, 4 August 2013; "Get real, banning lads' mags would patronise women", *Telegraph*, 13 June 2013

6 "Co-op threatens to withdraw sale of uncensored 'lads' mags'", *Guardian*, 29 July 2013

7 "The Co-operative pulls lads' mags and sport for not covering up", Co-operative Group news release, 9 September 2013

now stopped publishing. According to reports, the magazines had seen circulation drop with customers turning to content on mobile phones and social media.[8]

3. The effects of viewing sexualised images and pornography

A February 2010 report by Linda Papadopoulos referred to research showing that adults, including women, who viewed sexually objectifying images of women in the mainstream media were more likely to be accepting of violence:

The evidence gathered... suggests a clear link between consumption of sexualised images, a tendency to view women as objects and the acceptance of aggressive attitudes and behaviour as the norm.

"Both the images we consume and the way we consume them are lending credence to the idea that women are there to be used and that men are there to use them."[9]

Other impacts on young women and girls of "exposure to the sexualised female ideal" can include lower self-esteem, negative moods and depression.[10]

Reg Bailey's *Letting children be children report* (June 2011) said there was "a widespread and specific concern" about the display of magazines "with sexualised front covers or front pages on shelves where young children can see them":

"Although the content of such 'lads' mags' and newspapers is not pornography in the accepted sense (that is, not strong enough to be considered as 'top shelf' magazines), they trade on their sexualised content and many parents think retailers should treat them in the same way as

8 "FHM and Zoo closure marks end of lads' mags era", *Guardian*, 17 November 2015

9 Linda Papadopoulos, Sexualisation of young people: review, February 2010, p11

10 Ibid, p58

they treat pornography...."[11]

Pornography

The Government's February 2016 consultation on age verification for online pornography looked at some of the research on the harms of pornography.[12] The document said that "widespread exposure of minors to pornography before they would normally be sexually active may":

⇨ cause them distress;

⇨ impact on their relationships, development and

⇨ lead to the normalisation of the behaviours depicted in pornography.

A DCMS commissioned report on how children view pornography was published alongside the consultation.[13]

12 August 2016

⇨ The above information is reprinted with kind permission from the House of Commons Library. Please visit researchbriefings.parliament. uk for further information.

© *House of Commons Library 2017*

11 Department for Education, *Letting children be children: report of an Independent review of the commercialisation and sexualisation of childhood*, June 2011, p24

12 12 DCMS, *Child Safety Online: Age Verification for Pornography*, February 2016, Annex 2

13 Victoria Nash et al, *Identifying the Routes by which Children View Pornography Online: Implications for Future Policy-makers Seeking to Limit Viewing Report of Expert Panel for DCMS*, November 2015

Celebrity culture 'a threat to today's youth'

74% believe celebrity culture is having a negative impact on young people, though obesity and binge drinking are more commonly seen as threats.

'Thinspiration', a term used to describe things that inspire people to lose weight, has come under public scrutiny after husband of *Made in Chelsea* and *Celebrity Masterchef* star Millie Mackintosh used the word to describe a photo of her looking skinny on Twitter. The term is accused of encouraging bad eating habits and unhealthy body images, especially to young people and women, with some going as far as calling it pro-anorexic.

A new YouGov survey finds that the majority of British people (58%) think the term is inappropriate, including 52% of 18- 24-year-olds. Women are more likely than men to disapprove of the term, with 68% of women saying it is inappropriate compared to 50% of men.

The discussion over 'thinspiration' is part of a wider debate about how celebrity culture impacts British society, especially regarding body image and self-esteem. The survey shows that the majority of British people think that celebrity culture is having a negative effect on young people's (74%) and women's (72%) perceptions of their bodies; even 46% say it is having a negative effect for men.

Additionally, young people are more likely (32%) than average (26%) to say that celebrity culture is having a negative effect on how they perceive their own bodies, and are less likely (49%) than average (61%) to say they are happy with their weight and body image.

Other threats

The survey also asks which two or three problems are the biggest threats to 17- 18-year-olds today. Binge drinking and obesity are most commonly seen as the biggest threats, by 57% and 43%, respectively. Celebrity culture is one of the next most common choices, along with spending too much online and sexualised culture.

Only 8% see the eating disorders at the heart of the 'thinspiration' controversy as one of the biggest threats to 17- 18-year-olds.

The term 'thinspiration' started its life on pro-anorexia and pro-bulimia blogs, which fetishise certain aspects of skinniness, such as jutting hip bones, visible ribs and 'thigh gaps.' The word has now entered the more mainstream media, however, with it being prevalent on celebrity Twitter accounts and on the photo-sharing website Pinterest.

24 July 2014

⇨ The above information is reprinted with kind permission from YouGov. Please visit www.yougov.co.uk for further information.

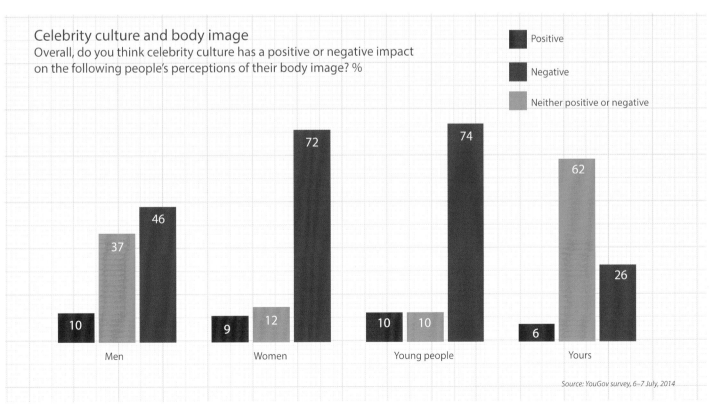

Celebrity culture and body image
Overall, do you think celebrity culture has a positive or negative impact on the following people's perceptions of their body image? %

Legend:
- Positive
- Negative
- Neither positive or negative

	Positive	Neither positive or negative	Negative
Men	10	37	46
Women	9	12	72
Young people	10	10	74
Yours	6	62	26

Source: YouGov survey, 6–7 July, 2014

Advert by 'ethical' clothing company banned for 'sexualising vulnerable children'

By Paul Wright

A series of adverts for an 'ethical' women's clothing brand have been banned following complaints that they sexualised vulnerable children. Two posters by Nobody's Child clothing company were found by the UK advertising regulators to breach codes concerning "harm and offence".

One ad showed a female model wearing a black jumpsuit and heeled shoes, sitting on the arm of a sofa with her breasts partially exposed and her mouth open. The other showed a woman sitting in what looked like an oversized chair wearing a tartan dress. Text on both adverts read: "nobody's child.com".

Several people complained to the Advertising Standards Authority (ASA) that the promotions "sexualised someone who they considered appeared to be a child". They said the model used looked under 18 and that the text "nobody's child" suggested the images portrayed were of vulnerable children.

The clothing company, which uses the slogan "ethical fashion" to promote what it says are responsible manufacturing practices, said the model used was 21 years old. In its opinion, she "was not sexualised and would not be perceived as being a child or vulnerable".

The company added: "The name Nobody's Child was intended to reflect the feeling their target audience experienced, that they were no longer children and were now their own person. The name was, therefore, recognition that their target audience had reached an age where they could make their own decisions and be their own people, rather than conveying vulnerability."

But in a ruling published on Wednesday (30 March), the ASA disagreed and ordered the adverts should never appear again. The watchdog said it considered the poses and gaze of the woman in the first advert were "mildly sexually suggestive", and that her pose in the other "suggested vulnerability".

It added: "We understood the model featured in the ads was 21 years of age but considered she appeared younger, and that when shown in conjunction with the prominent brand name 'nobody's child.com', would be regarded as appearing to be a child. We therefore concluded the ads portrayed a model who appeared to be a child in a way that was sexually suggestive and could be perceived as being vulnerable.

"We concluded that the ads were irresponsible and likely to cause serious or widespread offence. The ads must not appear again in their current form."

The ruling comes as the ASA continues to crack down on clothing companies using sexualised imagery of young-looking models. Last year, American Apparel was ordered to remove an online advert that portrayed a "sexualised" image of a model who "looked under 16 years of age".

It was the second time in six months that the company's ads had been banned in the UK. In September, the ASA banned adverts with images linked to the firm's 'School Days' and 'Back to School' ranges, one of which showed a woman in a short skirt bending over so that her underwear was visible.

The agency then said the images had the "potential to normalise predatory sexual behaviour" towards young women.

29 March 2016

⇨ The above information is reprinted with kind permission from *International Business Times*. Please visit www.ibtimes.co.uk for further information.

MP slams "too sexy" bra for children on sale at Matalan

An MP has slammed high street giant Matalan for selling a young girl's bra which says is "too sexualised" for children.

Sarah Champion, Shadow Minister for Preventing Abuse and Domestic Violence, says the £4 item of underwear, which is marketed by the firm as an "ideal first bra" for young girls, is "totally unsuitable".

The politician was contacted by a concerned parent about the bra which is sold in the two- to 13-years-old section via the Matalan website.

She said: "The bra is totally unsuitable for young girls. The design of the bra, which is black, with padding and a plunge-front, is too sexualised for any young child.

"Furthermore, despite advertising this as a 'teen' bra, the sizes available to buy are tiny, which means that the girls actually wearing the item could be younger than eight.

"Matalan are compounding this issue by selling the bra in the 2- to 13-years-old section."

She added: "The sale of clothes like this contributes to the sexualisation of children. These garments put children at risk and could be used in abusive images.

"It is tough enough for parents to protect their children from abuse without high street stores selling items that make their job more difficult.

"I am calling on Matalan to engage with the parent who contacted me and remove the item of clothing from their stores immediately."

A spokesman for Matalan said: "Since 2011 we have been working in conjunction with Mumsnet, where this sensitive issue was raised as part of their 'Let Girls be Girls' campaign.

"We purposely ensure that our girls bras are not sold to specific ages but are sold in sizes. They have been developed following customer feedback that girls want bras to protect their modesty at this sensitive age.

"The bras in question are not padded so as to enhance cleavage but are a smooth moulded shape to act as a modesty and comfort layer.

"We conduct thorough tests and speak to our customers for their feedback and as such, will always investigate any claims against Matalan regarding the suitability of our products. We take our commitment as a family business seriously, and Matalan is the only retailer in the UK to currently hold the Mumsnet Gold Award for being family friendly, an award we've held for the last three years."

13 May 2015

⇨ The above information is reprinted with kind permission from Hemel Today. Please visit www.hemeltoday.co.uk for further information.

Responsible retailers

Argos, Debenhams, George, John Lewis, M&Co, M&S, Next, Peacocks, Pumpkin Patch, Sainsbury's, Tesco and TK Maxx have all committed to applying the British Retail Consortium's (BRC) guidelines in designing, commissioning and marketing their Under 12s childrenswear ranges.

Examples of guidelines from the BRC include:

- Fabrics and cut should provide for modesty: for example, sheer fabrics without lining are not acceptable for childrenswear bodices or skirts

- Slogans and imagery must be age appropriate and without undesirable associations or connotations (for example, sexually suggestive, demeaning, derogatory or political material or phrasing that could be interpreted as such)

- Skirt and short length, neck/shoulder line and underwear shape need careful consideration, taking account of the stretch properties of the fabric used and the intended age group.

- Swimwear should provide for modesty, including when wet, and should be designed with children's needs specifically in mind.

Source: Responsible retailing: BRC childrenswear guidelines

No bra day slammed for "sexualising breast cancer" and "objectifying women"

By Rachel Moss

#NoBraDay is supposedly meant to raise public awareness about breast cancer, but not everyone is convinced that taking a nipple selfie is the best way to open discussion about a life-threatening disease.

The campaign has been slammed for "sexualising" breast cancer and "objectifying" women who take part.

Yet a lot of ladies are still keen to support the cause, posting images on social media.

It is unclear who started #NoBraDay and there doesn't appear to be a registered charity associated with the campaign.

However, a Facebook page named No Bra Day For Breast Cancer Awareness reads: "Ladies, free your breasts for 24 hours, our perkiness should not be hidden. It is time that the world see what we're blessed with.

"Your breasts might be colossal, adorable, miniature, full, jiggly, fancy, sensitive, glistening, bouncy, smooth, tender, still blossoming, rosy, plump, fun, silky, jello-like, fierce, jolly, nice, naughty, cuddly, sexy, perky, or drag the ground... YAY for boobies!"

Karen Dobres, who runs Loose Debra – a website featuring tips on how to look stylish while braless – does not think this Facebook page is the right way to raise breast cancer awareness.

She has a history of breast cancer in her family and finds the idea of #NoBraDay offensive.

"There seems to be a running theme this October, that as long as breast cancer awareness is mentioned, it doesn't matter what you do. The end (funding or added awareness) always justifies the means," she tells HuffPost UK Lifestyle.

"The writer appears to be very excited about the 'jiggly' nature of 'boobies'. I'm sorry but someone please tell me where taste and judgement come into this, because right now it sounds like a thinly veiled attempt to objectify women using the platform of breast cancer awareness. How low will we all sink?"

Dobres isn't the only one to criticise the campaign. Many others have accused #NoBraDay of "sexualising women" on social media.

The backlash against #NoBraDay comes after M&S's #ShowYourStrap campaign – which encourages people to snap a selfie with their bra strap on display and donate £3 to cancer research – received criticism from breast cancer survivors who said the disease "isn't pink and fluffy".

Feminist blogger Louise Pennington notes that both campaigns "reinforce the hyper-sexualised objectification of women's bodies".

"Women are already perfectly aware of their risk of breast cancer. There are countless campaigns exhorting women to check your breasts and there are massive amounts of fundraising from Moonwalks to Asda's pink branded eggs," she tells HuffPost UK Lifestyle.

"Men are squealing excitedly on Twitter about the possibility of seeing erect nipples on #NoBraDay. They certainly aren't interested in breast cancer research or how many women die each year from it.

"And, let's be honest here, these men don't want to see images of women who have actually had breast cancer – of mastectomy scars, hair loss or grieving families."

She goes on to say that we'll only really learn more about breast cancer by listening to women speak about the disease.

"Going without a bra or posting pictures of erect nipples isn't the reality of breast cancer," she says.

"If people want to raise awareness, talk to the women who have experienced it. Share their stories, not porno-fied images of the bodies of very young, thin women."

13 October 2015

⇨ The above information is reprinted with kind permission from The Huffington Post UK. Please visit www.huffingtonpost.co.uk for further information.

Ministry of Defence bans charity calendar amid fears it "sexualises" Royal Marines

The Royal Marines' butch calendar boys have been censored by military bosses, who have banned them from stripping off for a charity fundraiser.

The popular annual Go Commando calendar, which has raised hundreds of thousands of pounds to support Marine families, has been banned by the Ministry of Defence.

Members of Norton Fitzwarren-based 40 Commando had been sweating it out in the gym to tone up their muscles for the 2017 calendar – only to be stood down on the order of the MoD.

Scores of people getting excited about our boys from Norton Manor Camp flexing their muscles have taken to social media to protest at the high command flexing their muscles instead.

Former Royal Marine lieutenant colonel Kevin du Val, chairman of Go Commando, expressed his disappointment on the cover-up ruling.

He said: "The calendar is a great fundraiser and a bit of fun.

"Every year we have had to apply to the MoD to use service personnel, but this year they haven't given permission.

"They felt it was sexualising the Royal Marines. I don't agree with that. It's disappointing, but that's life."

"The Royal Marines' butch calendar boys have been censored by military bosses, who have banned them from stripping off for a charity fundraiser"

Thousands of copies of the calendar have been sold since it first appeared in 2012, its most successful year, when it raised more than £100,000 for Go Commando, which supports Royal Marines and their families.

Mr du Val added: "We've got to go with what the military have said.

"We'll see if we can change their minds, but it's too late for 2017.

"We're going to review it and might get some retired Royal Marines to pose for a calendar in 2018."

Retired Commandos posed for a previous calendar, although it failed to sell as well as other years.

Money from next year's calendar would have gone towards a £400,000 nursery and family community centre in Norton Fitzwarren available for use by the military and civilian population.

Among Facebook comments upset at the decision to block next year's calendar were: Lynne Brittany: "Could serving Marines hide their faces behind something, e.g. a basketball or tyre as the original ladies hid their assets behind cakes, etc. After all, be truthful, it's not faces being looked at."

"It's disappointing, but that's life"

Allison Bristow: "Very disappointing. The money it raises should be the main issue here! I fail to see the point of stopping a bit of fun that promotes an amazing group of people who are asked to put themselves in harms way to protect us all."

Simon Ferguson: "It's a shame you don't have the support of the Royal Marines command. They should hang their heads in shame."

7 October 2016

⇨ The above information is reprinted with kind permission from the *Somerset Country Gazette*. Please visit www.somersetcountrygazette.co.uk for further information.

© *Somerset Country Gazette 2017*

Sex on camera: the porn industry and its effects

An ex-worker blogs about her experiences in the sex industry, the reality behind the videos, and the effects of such material on the younger generation.

I have sampled the sex industry in its full and varied diversity. And in that time, I had taken two overdoses, been raped twice, consistently manipulated and became a functioning drunk. It's true to say, I am a rehabilitated abuse victim who gave her consent. The turning point was recognising I had to change for my child, now children, as well as furthering my education – which awarded me the ability to see the truth of what happened to me. I wasted most of my twenties in the industry, continuously pursuing the promise of a bit more money than the average wage, only to be left with no CV, and struggling with feelings of anger from sexual and emotional violation.

I must first point out that not all pornography is harmful, that sex on camera in itself is expression and can be artistic.

What I do have a problem with, is how easily misogynistic pornography can be accessed. This kind of porn, what I will refer to as 'gonzo' porn, worryingly commands approximately 98% of porn Internet traffic and is the current point of reference for sex education.

Women in gonzo porn are pitted as a debased object; voiceless and used and abused by men, who mock them and subject them to degrading acts. This is expression you may think, even if it isn't respectful. In some ways I'd agree with you – but because gonzo pornography is so easily accessed, it has permeated our everyday lives and distorted reality, with dangerous consequences...

Gonzo porn has replaced our understanding of the natural development of sex that exists in real relationships, between two people. It has sadly carved out a new identity for women who subconsciously embody the damaging 'slut' persona, feeling that this is the only way to 'impress' men. Porn also promotes self-sexualisation in very young girls, and has brainwashed boys and men into seeing women as fodder, not the multi-faceted people that they really are.

The word 'slut' is a common phrase in memes seen on many young teenagers, Facebook feeds and other social media, describing certain female classmates. The frequency of this unfair adjective is a new arrival, and goes hand in hand with the increase of degradation porn. Sure, when I was young there were girls who got intimate with more boys than others, but they weren't shamed to this extent. The children who grow up in the media-obsessed culture of today are experiencing an entirely new animal.

Girls are encouraged to self-sexualise through expectations of boys who watch porn regularly, but are then 'slut-shamed' for doing so. It's a trap, and one that society should be aware of for public health. Gonzo porn is

presented as edgy, and a reflection of freedom of expression. It is never presented in truth: as one gender's mass-scale violation.

If expression was really free in porn, then subgenres like 'alternative porn' would be more popular – where both genders are depicted as equal. The current porn industry is about control and humiliation of women, but boys and men are also being damaged by pornography; experiencing erectile dysfunction due to the bombardment of high speed graphic images. As a consequence, they also experience desensitisation to real sexual relationships.

The industries that make these representations don't care for one minute how they affect people. They only care about money. To remain healthy, it is our responsibility to maintain our sense of self-respect and to not be coerced into unwanted sex, or extreme acts just because porn has normalised them. The porn stars who act in these films are only doing it for money, and many of them are damaged people who take drugs and have had problematic upbringings.

I found myself in a bad place in my teens. I had a terrible relationship with my mother and left home at a very young age to stay with people I didn't really know. I starting seeing a man who was much older than myself, and then fell into the glamour industry. At first I thought it was fun – but very quickly I had developed a drinking habit to cope with the people who (in retrospect) used me. My world became very dark. Sure, there were some good things, like the money, but that eventually disappeared and all I was left with, were the scars of being sexually objectified.

I believe that sex workers should have workers' rights that prevent them from the coerced sexual abuse that happens time and time again. There are situations constantly cropping up on social media of girls complaining of being violated outside of shoots. I also believe that porn stars should be able to buy back images of themselves after ten years so they can transition in society more comfortably. The sex industry pays women more, as it needs its object to function, and women in the industry think they are getting a good deal, until they find themselves with no way of getting out. The permanence of their appearance on film leaves them with little prospect in corporate society. Women are not people in the sex industry, they are voiceless caricatures.

We don't know the true effects yet, as the Internet is relatively new, and I'm not dismissing its sheer awesomeness for one minute, but what I am fighting against is the graphic depiction of women as fodder. Are glamour models victims of a culture that sexualises women and young girls? What effects do these identities have on everyday women? Our children need more protection – both boys and girls. Glamour models are certainly not empowered like some say they are, but they wouldn't bite the hand that feeds them would they? If they weren't facilitating men's demands they wouldn't be of interest to these men.

The glamour model is an unhealthy construction and teaches women that they are decoration. They are merely brainwashed by a culture that disregards the best interests of humanity. We need to encourage connection and co-dependency, which means real rapport between boys and girls.

29 June 2016

⇨ The above information is reprinted with kind permission from Ditch The Label. Please visit www.ditchthelabel.org for further information.

Key facts

- According to a study, which looked at 15 websites of popular clothing stores in the US:

    - 69% of the clothing assessed in the study had only child-like characteristics

    - 4% had only sexualising characteristics, while

    - 25% had both sexualising and child-like characteristics

    - 1% had neither sexualised nor child-like characteristics. (page 1)

- A survey of more than 1,000 children aged 11–16 found that at least half had been exposed to online porn. Almost all (94%) of this group have seen it by age 14. (page 7)

- More than a third of boys aged 13- to 14-years-old who have seen porn want to copy the behaviour they saw. (page 7)

- 28% of 11- to 16-year-olds who have seen porn, saw it by accident, compared to 19% who searched for it alone. (page 7)

- 40% of girls have seen porn and feel more negatively about it than boys do. (page 8)

- 73 per cent sent of young people who sent nude images did so because they were asked to, either by their partner or someone unknown to them. (page 10)

- 59 per cent of the teens said they sent [nude selfies] because it was fun, exciting and a good way of flirting and meeting people. (page 10)

- 77% of people in the UK are familiar with the word 'selfie'. (page 11)

- At Ryde Academy on the Isle of Wight [in 2014] more than 250 girls were taken out of lessons because their skirts were too short. (page 15)

- Almost a third (29%) of 16- to 18-year-old girls say they have experienced unwanted sexual touching at school. (page 17)

- Nearly three-quarters (71%) of all 16- to 18-year-old boys and girls say they hear terms such as "slut" or "slag" used towards girls at schools on a regular basis. (page 17)

- 59% of girls and young women aged 13–21 said in 2014 that they had faced some form of sexual harassment at school or college in the past year. (page 17)

- The number of sexual offences reported in schools increased from 719 in 2011/12 to 1,955 in 2014/15 according to research obtained by Plan International UK from a number of Freedom of Information requests to UK police forces. (page 19)

- The Children's Society's annual review of young people's well-being found an estimated 283,000 girls aged 10–15 are not happy with their lives "overall". (page 20)

- Mintel reveals that half (50%) of all men say they don't pay much attention to advertising, whilst more than one quarter (26%) agree that men are sexualised in adverts just as much as women are. (page 26)

- 30% of men find adverts featuring female models clichéd, while 26% deem these sexist and another 15% find them patronising. (page 26)

- A YouGov survey [has found] that the majority of British people (58%) think the term 'thinspiration' is inappropriate, including 52% of 18- 24-year-olds. Women are more likely than men to disapprove of the term, with 68% of women saying it is inappropriate compared to 50% of men. (page 33)

- A YouGov survey shows that the majority of British people think that celebrity culture is having a negative effect on young people's (74%) and women's (72%) perceptions of their bodies; even 46% say it is having a negative effect for men. (page 33)

Androgynous

Gender neutral, as opposed to appearing strictly male or female. Androgyny usually implies a blend of both feminine and masculine attributes.

Beauty pageant

Beauty pageants are generally aimed at females (though similar events do exist for males). Contestants are judged on the combined criteria of physical beauty, personality and talent. There is, however, a tendency to focus on physical appearance above other characteristics. Some feel that beauty pageants are inappropriate for young girls because they promote a nation obsessed with looks. On the other hand, some believe that pageants promote confidence and self-esteem.

Commercial/Commercialisation

Exploiting something in order to gain money.

Commercial sexual exploitation of children

The Declaration and Agenda for Action against Commercial Sexual Exploitation of Children defines this as `a fundamental violation of children`s rights. It comprises sexual abuse by the adult and remuneration in cash or kind to the child or a third person or persons. The child is treated as a sexual object and a commercial object. The commercial sexual exploitation of children constitutes a form of coercion and violence against children, and amounts to forced labour and a contemporary form of slavery`. Commercial sexual exploitation of children may take the form of child abuse through the prostitution of children; using children to create images of child sex abuse (child `pornography`); providing children to visitors from overseas for the purpose of sexual abuse (child sex tourism), and child marriage where a child is used for sexual purposes in exchange for goods or services. Children who are sexually exploited in these ways may have been trafficked from another country for that purpose.

Gender stereotypes

Simplifying the roles, attributes and differences between males and females. Gender stereotyping encourages children to behave in ways that are considered most typical of their sex. For example, buying pink toys for girls and blue for boys, or limiting girls to playing with dolls and boys to toy-cars.

Grooming

Actions that are deliberately performed in order to encourage a child to engage in sexual activity. For example, offering friendship and establishing an emotional connection, buying gifts, etc.

Hypermasculinity

Parental control software/Network-level filters

Pornification

Very similar to sexualisation, the term pornification refers to the acceptance of sexualisation in our culture.

Sexualise/Sexualisation

To give someone or something sexual characteristics and associations. This refers to the idea that sex has become much more visible in culture and media today. Premature sexualisation of children involves exposure to sexual images and ideas at an age when they are emotionally unable to process such information. Implications include children having sex at a younger age, engaging in activities such as sexting, an increased likelihood of being groomed and has been linked to hypermasculine behaviour in boys and young men.

Watershed restrictions

A television watershed is in place to protect children from viewing material that is inappropriate for their age group. Adult content can only be shown after a certain time (or `after the watershed`). Some examples of adult content include graphic violence, nudity, swearing, gambling and drug use. Watershed times can vary around the world due to cultural difference. For example, in the UK the watershed for free-to-air television is between 21:00 and 05:30, whereas in the United States it begins at 22:00 and ends at 06:00.

Assignments

Brainstorming

➪ What is meant by the term 'sexualisation'?

➪ Name some industries in which 'sexualisation' is a problem.

➪ How does sexualisation negatively impact young people's mental health?

Research

➪ Visit a selection of high-street stores or supermarkets that sell children's clothes. Make a note of anything you find for children aged 14 or under that you consider to be 'sexualised' or inappropriate for its target age-group. Take photographs if the store manager allows you to do so. Share your findings with the rest of your class.

➪ Over the course of one week, make a note of the adverts you see on television, online and in magazines/newspapers that might be considered to sexualise men or women. If possible, cut out the advert or take a photograph of it. At the end of the week, tally up how many sexualised adverts you've seen featuring men vs. how many featuring women. Create a simple bar graph to demonstrate your findings and share with your class.

➪ Read the article 'Come on Rude Boy'… on pages 24 and 25, then conduct some research to find out whether music really has become more sexualised over time. Look back at music artists from the 50s, 60s, 70s, 80s, 90s and 00s and, if possible, interview older friends and relatives to help inform your opinion. Write a report summarising your findings and use pictures, adverts and newspaper articles to support your argument.

Design

➪ Choose one of the articles from this book and create an illustration that highlights the key themes of the piece.

➪ Design a leaflet highlighting the points raised by the educational guide to porn on pages eight and nine.

➪ Design an advert for a new 'wholesome' non-sexualised fashion brand for children under ten years of age. Think about the name of your brand, the kinds of clothes you will feature in order to remain 'on trend' but also age-appropriate. Your advert could be a web-banner, poster or social media ad.

Oral

➪ Why do you think the premature sexualisation of girls could lead to increased domestic violence against women? Discuss in small groups and feed back to the rest of the class.

➪ Choose one of the illustrations from the book and consider what message your chosen picture is trying to get across. How does it support, or add to, the points made in the accompanying article? Do you think it is successful?

➪ In small groups, discuss why you think young people share nude selfies.

➪ In pairs, list all the examples of sexualisation you can think of. For example, perfume adverts, children's clothes, etc. When you've finished, compare with your classmates.

➪ "School dress codes reinforce the message that women's bodies are dangerous." Debate this motion as a class with half of you arguing in favour and half arguing against.

➪ The Ministry of Defence recently banned a charity calendar featuring the Royal Marines' "butch calendar boys" for fears that it sexualised Marines. As a class, debate whether you believe the calendar should have been banned. In particular, think about how people may have reacted if it was a calendar featuring women instead of men.

Reading/writing

➪ Is sexualisation in video games only linked to female characters? Write a blog post exploring your opinion. Aim to write at least 500 words but remember it is a blog and style your language accordingly.

➪ After reading some of the topic articles as a starting point, write your own definition of the term 'sexualisation'. When you have finished, split into small groups and discuss your definitions. Feed back to the rest of the class.

➪ Write a definition of the term 'sexualisation'.

➪ Write a definition of the term 'sexual harassment'.

➪ Write an open letter to fitness instructors encouraging them to recognise and discourage the sexualisation of female fitness. Use your letter to highlight examples of how female fitness is sexualised, and discuss the effect it can have on women who want to partake in an exercise class. Use the article on page 23 for help.

➪ Write a blog post from either one of these two points of view, explaining why you feel the way you do:

➪ A mother who does not want her eleven-year-old daughter to wear make-up.

➪ A mother who allows her eleven-year-old daughter to wear make-up.

Acknowledgements

The publisher is grateful for permission to reproduce the material in this book. While every care has been taken to trace and acknowledge copyright, the publisher tenders its apology for any accidental infringement or where copyright has proved untraceable. The publisher would be pleased to come to a suitable arrangement in any such case with the rightful owner.

Images

All images courtesy of iStock except pages 16, 23, 27, 35 & 36 © Pixabay and page 21 © Ryan McGuire.

Icons

Icon on page 40 made by VectorsIcon from www.flaticon.com. Icon on page 41 made by Freepik from www.flaticon.com.

Illustrations

Don Hatcher: pages 14 & 34. Simon Kneebone: pages 1 & 37. Angelo Madrid: pages 10 & 30.

Additional acknowledgements

Editorial on behalf of Independence Educational Publishers by Cara Acred.

With thanks to the Independence team: Mary Chapman, Sandra Dennis, Jackie Staines and Jan Sunderland.

Cara Acred

Cambridge, September 2017

Changing Families

Editor: Tina Brand

Volume 329

Independence Educational Publishers

First published by Independence Educational Publishers

The Studio, High Green

Great Shelford

Cambridge CB22 5EG

England

ISBN-13: 978 1 86168 780 7

Printed in Great Britain

Zenith Print Group